Modernity and Responsibility:
Essays for George Grant

What is it to be modern? How does the world look through the eyes of a modern? Is it possible to bring the sensibility of the non-modern to bear on the world around one? If so, how?

The essays in this volume consider these and a number of related questions in an attempt to determine how a thoughtful individual can understand and act justly in the world of modernity. The authors stand firmly and deeply in modernity, but they are profoundly aware of the classical and the Judaeo-Christian traditions that the modern world has largely discarded and of non-Western traditions that ask profound questions about the nature of man and his role in the universe. They are willing to ask difficult and critical questions about traditional thought and about the assumptions, often tacit, of modernity.

The essays explore the problematic nature of the concept of transcendence in modern social and political philosophy. They start with an analysis of Spinoza's use of biblical criticism to separate political philosophy and divine revelation, and explore the impact of the rise of naturalistic individualism in the North Atlantic world. A discussion of the role of the transcendent and of traditional philosophy in the East helps the reader to gain a deeper understanding of the process of secularization in the West. The issue of moral responsibility is shown to be greatly influenced by the existence of the concept of transcendence, and philosophy and the apocalyptic tradition form the basis of attempts to bridge the gulf between the traditional and the modern, secular view of the world.

These essays show that the quest for the grounds of responsible action requires a thorough-going critique of modernity that looks not only at the modern world, but beyond it, to the traditions that formed and still inform it, and to the experience of other cultures that are also facing the processes we already take for granted.

EUGENE COMBS is a professor in the Department of Religious Studies and an associate dean of social sciences at McMaster University.

EUGENE COMBS, editor

Modernity
and responsibility

ESSAYS FOR GEORGE GRANT

UNIVERSITY OF TORONTO PRESS
TORONTO   BUFFALO   LONDON

© University of Toronto Press 1983
Toronto Buffalo London
Reprinted in paperback 2015

ISBN 978-0-8020-2445-9 (cloth)
ISBN 978-1-4426-3930-0 (paper)

Canadian Cataloguing in Publication Data

Main entry under title:
Modernity and responsibility : essays for George Grant
Bibliography: p.
Includes index.
ISBN 978-0-8020-2445-9 (bound) ISBN 978-1-4426-3930-0 (pbk.)
1. Responsibility – Addresses, essays, lectures.
2. Ethics – Addresses, essays, lectures. 3. Tradition
(Philosophy) – Addresses, essays, lectures.
4. Grant, George, 1918–   I. Combs, Eugene, 1934–
II. Grant, George, 1918–
BJ1451.M62 1984   170   C83-099026-7

Cover illustration: *Woman, Jockey and Horse* [1952] by Alex Colville
(private collection), reproduced by kind permission of the artist

Contents

vi Contents

Preface

This volume has been developed from a collection of essays presented to George Grant on the occasion of his sixtieth birthday in 1978. Its publication witnesses Grant's sixty-fifth birthday. The book is not directly about Grant, his life and thought, but it is indirectly about him in that it explores matters that have interested him and held his attention throughout his life. The volume is about matters that matter and so tries to honour and represent George Grant's thought.

The authors of the essays that make up the book have each learned from Grant without having become imitators of him. This would please him, for Grant has resisted belonging to a school or founding a school, on the ground that matters of deepest concern are too subtle and complex to be reduced to a school, a style, or a method and too important to be recited by epigones. But the essays belong to Grant, not only in that they were a gift to him but also in that they arise from, and take their focus from, the articulate, profound, and moving thought that is characteristic of his writings. The model for the authors' efforts has been George Grant's efforts.

The authors of these essays stand firmly and deeply in modernity, but with an awareness and memory of traditions modernity has largely discarded and with a sense of responsibility to the past. If they have not been wholly shaped by those traditions and their meanings, neither have they been entirely shaped by modernity, and this is precisely because their recollection of tradition, or their striving to recall it, is so keen. They do not flinch from confronting the traditions critically or from confronting modernity with the insights of those traditions. They have in common their affirmation, which is the affirmation of the book as a whole (as it is of Grant's work), that it is irresponsible to fail to examine modernity critically and that the ground for criticism and responsibility is not to be found within modernity itself, any more than it is to be found within any one tradition. Responsibility, the authors assert, takes precedence over the modernity in which we live. Modernity indeed provides the setting for our responsibility, as the traditions have provided earlier settings, but it does not, cannot, and must not define or limit it.

The tension between modernity and responsibility (a potentially creative tension inherent in the priority of responsibility) is explored by each of the authors from a different stance and using a different model or frame of reference. Thus the opening essay, by Combs, examines that early moment in the rise of modernity when one major foundation of human ordering in the West (namely, the Bible) was subject to critical analysis by Spinoza from the standpoint of his naturalism and was thereby shown to be inadequate for continuing to govern human life. Spinoza thus represents and symbolizes a characteristic feature of modernity: its own critique of the past and its attempt to found human ordering apart from, or through a transforming interpretation of, the teachings of the great philosophical and religious traditions of the past. An unusual aspect of this essay, at least in the context of this volume, is that the particular moment in the rise of modernity to which our attention is drawn involves a tension between a traditional concept of the world as historical and contingent and an early modern concept of it as eternal and necessary. The concept of history with its related notions of progression and development is, paradoxically, more readily associated with modernity than is the concept of the eternal. It is appropriate that the first essay invites readers to ponder the relationship of modernity, nature, and history, through the observation in the essay of the paradox that in contrast to Spinoza's view, the biblical account of creation says that nature is not eternal, but has a history.

Grant, we may suppose, would respond to this essay with his own critique of the biblical view. He might argue that Spinoza is in some respects (and laudably) unrepresentative of modern thought. But the central concern of the essay, which is to explore two distinct foundations of political ordering, one from a great religious tradition and one from an exponent of the kind of thinking that has characterized modernity, is Grant's concern also. Time and again the question must be asked: on what is human society best founded? The attempt to answer is an intrinsic part of responsibility and is properly urged in this book.

Doull's essay sees the tension of our political time as being between the rational and the natural. He identifies rationalism closely with classical and pre-modern Christian thought, whereas naturalistic individualism he sees as a characteristic of modernity easily observed, at least in the West. Doull suggests that the rational and natural are more than in tension now; they are in direct conflict. This is in contrast to the Christian European culture of the past, in which a harmony between reason and nature was achieved by the subordination of the natural through a 'long correction and education of humanity.' Doull sees Marxism as epitomizing, but not solely responsible for, the reversal of this educative process and the acceptance of naturalism on a large scale in the modern world. Reason (other than abstract, impersonal, technological reason) is understood by moderns as an improper alienation from the natural and bodily, rather than as a proper corrective to nature. Some manifestations of this decadent understanding are, Doull says, the poorly thought-out movements for various 'natural' human and ecological rights and a view of the 'real' church, state, or other institution as local and particular rather than as universal and ideal. Doull finds grounds for hope, however, in some aspects of this modernism, notably the increasingly obvious failure of modern institutions and the adoption of new cultural models that may have the potential for rational re-education. He seems to see a smaller hope in the possibility that Canadians, through being drawn more strongly than Americans to the older traditions, may eventually reject technological naturalism and return to rationalism. 'To regain a knowledge of this thought ... appears to be the principal intellectual work of the present time.'

In Arapura's essay, the tension is between the transcendent and the immanent, representing the Eastern traditional and the modern respectively. Arapura points out that a concept of transcendence is at the very heart of philosophical thought, and that the rejection of the concept of transcendence by moderns is a rejection of philosophy itself. This is so despite the powerful influence of Kant's condemnation of pretensions to knowledge of things-in-themselves, the ultimately real. What is often overlooked in Kant is that 'he left the real in its complete aura of sacredness' without rejecting it at all. In this respect he was in accord with the Vedanta, which also sees the Ultimately Real as unknowable. What is quite different about much modern quasi-philosophy is its rejection of the transcendent as reality, not just as knowable. For the modern, says Arapura, there is no reality other than that which is illuminated by human research, and no concept of an illumination that is independent of human perception with its inherent limitations. This is in marked contrast to the Vedantic teaching that Brahman is the source of knowledge of all else – that the transcendent is that which makes possible any understanding of the immanent and which indeed underlies the immanent and gives it shape. Moreover, acknowledgment of transcendent reality involves a certainty that is completely inimical to the immanentist modern consciousness. We have special need of such certainty in our age, Arapura says, since 'because of transcendental certainty the Categorical Imperative will be able to bring forth noble deeds. This age especially cries for noble deeds.'

The polarities that Jan explores in his essay are the Confucian tradition on the one hand and technology as it has affected Chinese life and thought on the other. Confucian teaching is primarily concerned with the relationships between human beings, while technology ignores this vital aspect of life in favour of the relationship between man and nature. Moreover, traditional Chinese life is characterized by co-operation and harmony, whereas competition and conflict are basic to technology; the imposition of the latter on Chinese life is thus intrinsically problematic, not only in the results but also in the process. Like Doull, Jan sees hope for China in the recognition of the dilemma posed by the inability to return to the past and the inappropriateness for China of a Western-style technological future. This recognition can be a spiritual as well as an intellectual awakening, involving a new sense of human responsibility for nature as well as for humanity.

The next essay is the one which most directly addresses the subject of the volume as a whole. Smith addresses the topic of moral responsibility in a radical way, i.e. by exploring the very roots and meaning of the term. He finds that although specific understandings of the nature of responsibility, such as judgment and retribution, are culturally and historically limited, the concept that the word tries to express transcends all the metaphors associated with it. Moreover the moral sense is deeper, Smith suggests, than the sense that we will be held accountable for our actions; indeed, while that sense of accountability prevails there is no room for the highest religious experience: redeeming grace. Grace overcomes retribution and judgment and responsibility; it is grace that the modern world cries out for so urgently, without knowing, even, the object of its yearning.

What place does this thesis have in a volume focused on responsibility in the modern context? First, it belongs here because it studies the nature of responsibility as something that must be understood before it can be carried out in our own or any other situation. Second, it affirms that a sense of responsibility is the basis of human decency, that without such a sense our actions will necessarily fall below the level that can properly be called human. That modernity may largely lack such a sense is a call to action among those who possess it. Third, Smith puts to us the possibility that despite its failure to be responsible, modernity (our lives and their context) may yet be saved. Thus his essay is properly placed in juxtaposition with those that express a more tentative hope for responsible change, including the one that follows.

Penelhum, in the next essay, looks at the differences between a world informed by faith (specifically by Christianity) and one that, like Western modernity, is secular in its understanding of reality. He undertakes to describe how the world appears to Christian eyes and then shows how radically our culture has moved away from this view. The move has been one, Penelhum says, that subtracts from the traditional view, makes it less complete, rather than being an additive process by which modernity has gained understanding, through science for example. The God-dimension has been lost by moderns, and their consequently hazy view of life has not yet been blessed by a restorative vision. The deprived outlook that results from the loss of the transcendent recognizes its deprivation when it sees the world as absurd, i.e. lacking in rational meaning. However, suggests Penelhum, a further, unrecognized deprivation occurs with advancing secularization, as the sense of absurdity fades.

Another aspect of secularization is the prevalence of moral anarchy, and Penelhum finds the seeds of this anarchy, paradoxically, in Christianity itself, though there has been distortion and perversion in the secular use of Christian ideas. Jesus taught that individual moral judgment, or conscience, overrides law, and that explicit knowledge of law is even unnecessary to good moral action. In the secular world, these teachings are perverted into disregard for moral teaching and into arrogant moral individualism. Both the loss of the transcendent and the loss of moral absolutes have contributed to modern anxiety and despair, and Penelhum underlines the inevitability of anxious, often despairing, uncertainty in those secular persons who cannot affirm that through an Almighty God all will, ultimately, be well. The relation between faith and secularity is one of fundamental psychological opposition rather than one of inconsequential differences of belief; the person of faith sees the world, and thus moves within it, in a way quite clearly other than does the unbeliever for whom life's ultimate outcome is ever in question.

The six essays dealing with the various tensions between modernity and tradition are followed by Rotstein's 'The World Upside Down,' the volume's concluding piece. Appropriately for a seventh essay, this one is quite distinct from those that precede it, in that it attempts the difficult task of seeing not the difference between the modern world-view and another, but rather the common thread that runs through Marxist modernity and a specific tradition, apocalyptic Christianity. Instead of seeing Marxism and Christianity as mirror-images (a fairly conventional view, endorsed, Rotstein points out, by Marx himself and by Reinhold Niebuhr, among others) Rotstein sees Marxism as a spinning out of the same mythical thread. The story that is told over and over again, from Moses to Marx, is the story of a change of mind, an overturning not only of an established order but of the way in which it was seen – above all, of the way in which oppression and bondage were understood. The change of mind is, typically, complete and sudden, a true turning upside-down of the previously held ideal of community and of that which is conducive to the ideal. Rotstein believes that a capacity for further such revolution is inherent in all apocalyptic movements, by virtue of the schism that exists between the apocalyptic vision and the conditions of historical existence. He raises the possibility that this intrinsic revolutionary tendency should be integrated into theological anthropology: a new theology of revolution, more radical than any liberation theology, might be the outcome.

In all seven essays, including the last, the authors present the readers with the need for responsibility within modernity and with the tensions involved in the attempt to reach responsibility. Each writer urges an endeavour that none suggests will be easy. My own urging would have biblical scientists ponder the biblical foundations of right political ordering; as if this were not a sufficiently massive task for specialists, I would press on all those who are concerned with matters that matter that they take seriously once more the relation between theology and political science. I urge, in fact, what I take to be the Grantian endeavour upon the readers of this book. Doull cries out for a return to rationalism, Arapura for recollection of transcendental certainty, Jan for a new appreciation of tradition. All three are concerned with the appropriation of ancient values by moderns, which cannot happen easily or without a heightening of the tensions already present. Smith presents to us the wonderful possibility that these daunting tasks may yet not daunt us if we are *graced*. Penelhum echoes the thought that our whole outlook may be different when we have glimpsed transcendent reality, and Rotstein brings us full circle by both giving us a task, to think revolution, and suggesting that in the doing of it we are graced already, for human consciousness by nature knows about turning the world upside-down.

Responsibility must always give rise to tasks of thought or action, as readers of Grant's work have come to appreciate. Our work is dedicated to a philosopher whose political prudence arises from responsible thinking, from which he has refused to 'squeak in the gab of the age,' to quote from the poem by Dennis Lee in this volume. The dedication comes from gratitude that each one of us has been able to appreciate this responsible thinker and has learned from him. We hope that our essays, our thoughts, are responsible in turn and that they will stimulate further thinking on these matters that matter.

EUGENE COMBS

MODERNITY AND RESPONSIBILITY

Acknowledgments

I am happy to acknowledge that this book has been published with the help of a grant from the Social Science Federation of Canada, using funds provided by the Social Sciences and Humanities Research Council of Canada, and a grant from the McMaster Arts Research Board, McMaster University, Hamilton, Ontario.

I wish to express my gratitude to the following persons for their assistance in bringing this volume to be: Dr Alvin Lee, president and vice-chancellor, McMaster University, for providing funds with which I originally initiated the project to honour George Grant on his birthday; Dr Craig McIvor, professor emeritus, McMaster University, who, when he was dean of the Faculty of Social Sciences, provided additional funds to reproduce the original set of essays which went as a gift to George Grant; Grace Gordon, senior secretary, Department of Religion, McMaster University, for typing, telephoning, and helping with various arrangements well beyond her normal duties; and Anne Yarwood, an associate of mine at McMaster, who studied these essays and discussed them with me and greatly helped me in formulating the preface.

I am grateful to the editors of *Canadian Journal of Political and Social Theory / Revue canadienne de théorie politique et sociale* for permission to reprint in substantially the same form Abraham Rotstein's essay, 'The World Upside Down,' which appeared in Vol 2 No 2 (Spring–Summer / Printemps–Été 1978), pp 5–30. I am grateful also to Alex Colville who allowed a copy of his painting *Truck Stop* to serve as his contribution to this volume. Finally, I wish to acknowledge that Dennis Lee's poem appeared in *The Gods*, published by McClelland and Stewart (Toronto 1979), pp 29–32.

Alex Colville
Truck Stop 1966
Acrylic polymer emulsion
91.4 × 91.4 cm
Museum Ludwig, Cologne

DENNIS LEE

The Gods

I

Who, now, can speak of gods –
their strokes and carnal voltage,
old ripples of presence   a space ago
archaic eddies of being?

Perhaps a saint could speak their names.
Or maybe some
noble claustrophobic spirit,
crazed by the flash and
vacuum of modernity,
could reach back, ripe for
gods and a hot lobotomy.
But being none of these, I sit
bemused by the sound of the words.
For a man no longer moves
through coiled ejaculations of
meaning;
we dwell within
taxonomies, equations, paradigms
which deaden the world and now in our
heads, though less in our inconsistent lives,
the tickle of cosmos is gone.
Though what would a god be *like* –

would he shop at Dominion?
Would he know about DNA molecules? and keep little
haloes, for when they behaved?
... It is not from simple derision
that the imagination snickers. But faced with an alien
reality it
stammers, it races & churns
for want of a common syntax and
lacking a possible language
who, now, can speak of gods? for random example
a bear to our forebears, and even to
grope in a pristine hunch back to that way of being on earth
is nearly beyond me.

II

And yet –
in the middle of one more day, in a clearing maybe   sheer
godforce
calm on the lope of its pads
furred   hot-breathing   erect, at ease, catastrophic
harsh waves of stink, the
dense air clogged with its roaring and
ripples of power fork through us:
hair gone electric   quick
pricklish glissando, the
skin   mind skidding, balking is
HAIL
and it rears foursquare and we are jerked and owned and
forgive us   and
brought to a welter, old
force & destroyer and
do not destroy us!
or if it seems good,
destroy us.

Thus, the god against us in clear air.
And there are gentle gods –
as plain as
light that
rises from lake-face,
melding with light
that skips like a stepping-stone spatter
down to
evoke it
till blue embraces blue, and lake and sky
are miles of indigenous climax –
such grace in the shining air.

All gods, all gods and none of them
domesticated angels, chic of spat & wing
on ten-day tours of earth. And if
to speak of 'gods' recalls those antique
wind-up toys, forget the gods as well:
tremendum rather,
dimension of otherness, come clear
in each familiar thing – in
outcrop, harvest, hammer, beast and
caught in that web of otherness
we too endure & we
worship.
Men lived among that force, a space ago.

Or,
whirling it reins into phase through us, good god it can
use us, power in tangible
dollops invading the roots of the
hair, the gap behind the neck,
power to snag, coax bully exalt into presence
clean gestures of meaning among the traffic of earth,
and until it lobs us aside, pale snot poor

                              rags we
                    also can channel the godforce.
                                        Yet still not
            abject: not
                    heaven & wistful hankering – I mean
                the living power, inside
                                and, that sudden that
                    plumb!
                Men lived in such a space.

                              III

        I do say gods.
        But that was time ago, technology
                    happened and what has been withdrawn
        I do not understand, the absent ones,
            though many then too were bright & malevolent and
                    crushed things that mattered,
    and where they have since been loitering I scarcely comprehend,
            and least of all can I fathom, you powers I
        seek and no doubt cheaply arouse and
                    who are you?
            how I am to salute you, nor how contend with your being
    for I do not aim to make prize-hungry words (and stay back!) I want
                    the world to be real and
                    it will not,
        for to secular men there is not given the glory of tongues, yet it is
            better to speak in silence than squeak in the gab of the age
                and if I cannot tell your terrifying
            praise, now Hallmark gabble and chintz nor least of all
                what time and dimensions your naked incursions
                    announced, you scurrilous powers yet
                still I stand against this bitch of a shrunken time
                            in semi-faithfulness
    and whether you are godhead or zilch or daily ones like before
                you strike our measure still and still you
                        endure as my murderous fate, though I
            do not know you.

EUGENE COMBS

Spinoza's method of biblical interpretation and his political philosophy

Spinoza is known as the founder of modern biblical criticism[1] and the founder of liberal democracy.[2] His foundational writing is *A Theologico-Political Treatise* (hereafter *TPT*).[3] Biblical scholars who acknowledge Spinoza as the founder of biblical criticism pay little attention to his political thought, as if it were distinct from his account of the Bible;[4] political scholars who acknowledge the importance of Spinoza in stating the modern theory of democracy pay little attention to, if they do not actually ignore, his account of the Bible.[5]

The purpose of this essay is to demonstrate the connection between Spinoza's biblical criticism and his political philosophy.[6] The first section examines Spinoza's intention in *TPT* to prove the compatibility of the Bible and philosophy by radically distinguishing their realms and thereby to invoke the Bible in support of his political philosophy. The second section isolates and articulates both the theological and political purpose of Spinoza's biblical criticism through a detailed analysis of his three main arguments. The third and final section examines more closely the role of Spinoza's biblical criticism in correlating his view of nature and his political thought. The essay concludes by alluding to a form of biblical criticism that would direct itself toward explicating the political corollary of the biblical account of creation.

I

Political philosophy is a branch of philosophy.[7] Philosophy is the quest for universal knowledge of the whole, or of all things. 'Quest for knowledge of "all things" means quest for knowledge of God, the world, and man – or rather quest for knowledge of the natures of all things: the natures in their totality are "the whole."[8] Political philosophy is a quest for knowledge of the nature of political things. Political things make claims to be judged by the standards of goodness or badness, justice or injustice. Political philosophy seeks to know the true standards. 'Political philosophy is the attempt truly to know both the nature of political things and the right, or the good, political order.'[9]

Political philosophy differs from political thought in that the latter is the reflection on or the exposition of political ideas, although the ideas may arise solely from a firmly held conviction or a myth; political philosophy, by contrast, is set in motion and kept in motion by the fundamental difference between conviction and knowledge. 'A political thinker who is not a philosopher is primarily interested in, or attached to, a specific order of policy; the political philosopher is primarily interested in, or attached to, the truth.'[10]

Political philosophy differs from political theory, which offers comprehensive reflections on the political situation that lead to the suggestion of broad policy. By appealing to public opinion political theory assumes principles that can be questioned by political philosophy or states premises as given without justification in reference to what is true. Justification of premises by reference to what is true is the work of political philosophy.

Political philosophy differs from political theology in that the latter bases its political teachings on divine revelation, or the Bible. In its search for what is true, political philosophy limits itself to what is accessible to the unassisted human mind. Nevertheless, political philosophy and political theology have this in common: they both assume the possibility of a final account of the whole and thus the knowledge of what political order is most consistent with that whole. Political philosophy and political theology differ in respect to their source of knowledge.

In classical times and through the medieval period this difference did not express itself in the form of the complete rejection of the claims of one in favour totally of the claims of the other. Largely, the relation of political philosophy and political theology was expressed through various degrees of synthesis, or at least a prudent respect of one leading to silence about the claims of the other.

Modern thought is in part the rise of a new political philosophy that is a critique of classical political philosophy and political theology in the name of and from the standpoint of a new realism that appeals not to the ideal republic or the kingdom of God, but to base instincts such as fear and pride for the foundation of human ordering.[11] The founders of the new political philosophy were Machiavelli and Hobbes. Spinoza, a late contemporary of Hobbes's, took up the claims of the new political philosophy but with in mind a particular problem, the classical problem of the relation of political philosophy and political theology, or the relation of Athens and Jerusalem.[12] In the language of *TPT*, Spinoza took up the problem of the relation of reason and revelation.

Spinoza's overall purpose in *TPT* is to demonstrate that reason and revelation are two distinct realms, each having a legitimate but definite and circumscribed place in human ordering. What Spinoza seeks to achieve is not a synthesis of reason and revelation but a total separation; yet he seeks a separation of a certain kind which resembles synthesis, namely the ascendancy of reason in determining human ordering on the grounds that revelation can be shown to be totally compatible with reason, supporting the dictates of reason by, in effect, influencing the masses to act in accord with the teaching of reason. In Spinoza's analysis, reason may be depicted as a kind of calm and stately teacher, whose thought only a blessed few can directly understand, and revelation may be depicted as a preacher of fiery imagination and persuasiveness, who, acting in accord with the thought of reason, orders and controls the masses through the language of revelation. Revelation, or the Bible, by this depiction, is not thought, having nothing to do with philosophical truth, speculation, metaphysics: it is, at best, a book inducing men to act decently.

Spinoza's is a philosophico-political critique of the Bible inasmuch as he employs a certain philosophical account of the whole and its political corollary to reject the theologico-political claim that the Bible provides knowledge of the whole and of the right or good political ordering of men. That Spinoza entitles his work a 'theologico-political' treatise requires explanation. His argument is against the Bible insofar as the Bible, in particular the Pentateuch, is held by political theologians to be a theologico-political document, that is, insofar as the Pentateuch is said to be a word from God and about God concerning the whole of things that leads to a way of living, a certain way of ordering men.[13] Spinoza would rid the Bible of its theologico-political status, assigning it the new role of confirming what reason knows and influencing in behalf of reason unreasonable men. He would place in its stead his philosophical account of the whole and its corollary political ordering; in short, Spinoza would have his philosophico-political treatise be a theologico-political treatise. The sequence of the Pentateuch itself may be said to be 'theologico-political,' i.e. it speaks of God first as creator and second as law-giver. In replacing it, Spinoza likewise arranges his work in a theologico-political manner, arguing in the first part what he takes to be true regarding the word from God and about God and in the second part what he takes to be politically true, or the true political ordering. There remains to be explained the presence of the chapters – at the centre of *TPT* – on his proposed method of biblical interpretation.

The basic rationale of *TPT* is expressed in the title, which asserts that the writing first states theological concerns that are followed by and related to political concerns. These concerns can be perceived, on close analysis, in two separate parts of the book. In the opening part, chapters 1–6, Spinoza critically discusses the biblical concepts of prophecy, law, chosenness, and miracles, by way of setting forth what he takes to be the highest truth known to philosophy, namely the eternal necessity of things. In the final part, chapters 16–20, Spinoza gives an account of what he takes to be the best political ordering of men, namely the ordering that overcomes but is initiated by the state of nature itself. In the middle part, chapters 7–15, to which biblical scholars especially refer in noting Spinoza's contribution to biblical criticism,[14] Spinoza details what he takes to be the correct procedure for reading the Bible, or, as he informs his readers in the preface, the way that will 'set this forth categorically and exhaust the whole question,' i.e. what is the central teaching of the Bible?

In seeking to understand the relation of Spinoza's biblical criticism to his political philosophy we must understand then the course of his entire argument, in particular the relation of its three parts.

II

THE FIRST ARGUMENT (CHAPTERS 1–6)

Spinoza's first argument consists in analysing the concept of prophecy or revelation, the work of the prophets, the vocation of the Hebrews, the foundation and function of law, and the concept of miracles from the standpoint of his leading philosophical proposition: 'Everything takes place by the power of God. Nature herself is the power of God under another name, and our ignorance of the power of God is co-extensive with our ignorance of Nature.'[15] The issue at stake for Spinoza is most apparent in considering to whom his argument is addressed.[16]

The course of his argument in the first section is occasioned by his primary and secondary audiences. In the preface he addresses his work to and describes it as a guide for the potential philosopher, the 'Philosophical Reader,' whose thought is blocked by the belief that reason is subservient to revelation, as known through the Bible.[17] Spinoza does not directly address the masses, 'the rest of mankind,' whom he asks not to read his treatise, lest it displease or mislead them. However, inasmuch as he knows that he cannot keep *TPT* out of their hands he writes secondarily with them in mind. Spinoza's argument, to be persuasive, must be delicate because what in his view reason teaches to be the highest truth, the co-existence of God and Nature, or the eternal necessity of nature, is radically opposed by what political theology alleges to be the highest teaching of the Bible, or what was regarded as the highest by both Christian and Jewish tradition, namely, the creation of all things by God.[18] According to this view, most simply stated, God is prior to and is the maker of nature, standing over, above, and against it.[19] Face to face with Spinoza's view, the biblical account of creation says that nature is not eternal, but has a history. To argue against the doctrine of creation as such would be for Spinoza to honour it as a speculative doctrine worthy of philosophical consideration; this course would in turn go against his separating reason and revelation into two absolutely distinct realms. A direct argument would also undermine his appeal to the masses, most of whom would believe in the doctrine of creation as taught both in the synagogue and the church. Spinoza's strategy, which unfolds in the sequence of the first six chapters, is to argue that concepts that lead to and presuppose the doctrine of creation do not have their base in the Bible or can be explained away as having arisen from a misinterpretation of biblical teaching. By this plan the doctrine of creation is attacked not directly, but indirectly through what Spinoza puts forth as subordinate corollaries to that doctrine. It should be noted that the first argument of Spinoza's critique of the Bible does not presuppose or require his procedure for reading the Bible. That procedure he is to set forth only after he has shown that the biblical account of creation is compatible with the philosophical account of nature. It is not his procedure that establishes in his mind the correct teaching of the Bible, but his leading philosophical proposition.

Those concepts that build toward the idea of creation Spinoza states in their simplest if not oversimplified and crude forms, summarized as follows. God has spoken to men through prophets, by means of prophecy. God has spoken especially to the Hebrews; the chief word that God has spoken to the Hebrews is law, that is, *torah* or guidance as to proper living. Law presupposes that the people are to act by divine instruction, not by nature, or by necessity. This condition in turn presupposes that God acts upon nature, or even contrary to nature; that is, that God performs miracles. For God to perform miracles in this manner is for God to be creator, that is, to be over and above and not bound to nature. Thus, the fundamental teaching of the Bible is that God is creator.

Against these concepts Spinoza's arguments take on the following broad form. Prophecy is a fleeting and uncertain activity of the imagination; it is not the activity of sure mental laws. As such, prophecy or the work of the prophets arises from and is aimed at levels of intelligence best described as ignorant and of conflicting opinion. It therefore follows that 'we must by no means go to the prophets for knowledge, either of natural or of spiritual phenomena.'[20] In other words, prophecy, or revelation, or the Bible, cannot and should not serve as the foundation of proper human ordering. In particular, the teaching of the prophets and the entire Hebrew people cannot be regarded as having a special or unique prominence in regard to thinking that leads to human ordering. The 'laws' of the Bible are in fact of two kinds: divine laws, i.e. those that are in accord with nature, inasmuch as God and nature are co-extensive; and ceremonial laws, having to do solely with the regulation of worship, diet, and mundane life of a particular people at a particular time and a particular place, namely the time and place of the Hebrews when the Bible was composed. Above all, there is nothing unique or special about the Hebrews and their laws; the laws are of human, not divine origin. Revelation has not actually taken place in the sense of a miracle, defined as any contravention of nature.

The sum of these six chapters is that the Bible itself only seems to talk about or to be revelation; the true character of biblical writing appears under the exposure of the philosophical teaching that all things come to be naturally, not divinely (if by 'divinely' one understands anything contrary to nature). The traditional understandings of prophecy, of the chosen people, of law and miracles, and ultimately of the doctrine of creation collapse under the weight of the view that all things exist by nature; and so subtle and delicate is Spinoza's first argument that he is able to demonstrate that the Bible itself agrees with his primary and leading philosophical proposition.

THE SECOND ARGUMENT (CHAPTERS 7–15)

The first argument of TPT states that the authors of the Bible did not think properly or intelligently, because they were not philosophers. Instead, the authors were prophets, people of vivid imagination, not of certain thought. The second argument of TPT, the more famous part from the standpoint of biblical criticism, is a critique of the Bible which states that its authors did not write or preserve their writings properly, or rationally, again because they were not philosophers; nevertheless, the axioms or basic teachings of the Bible can be discerned underneath the apparent disorderly composition, just as one can discover the laws of nature underneath the apparent disorder of nature. Accordingly, Spinoza argues, the Bible is to be interpreted on analogy with the interpretation of nature. 'I may sum up the matter by saying that the method of interpreting Scripture does not widely differ from the method of interpreting nature – in fact, it is almost the same.'[21] This method Spinoza takes to be in direct antithesis to the methods taking their cue from what he calls 'theological prejudice,' or the view that God has spoken through and revealed His will through the Bible.[22]

By Spinoza's reckoning there are two kinds of books, those dealing with subject matter which by its nature is easily perceived, whereof the understanding can give a clear and distinct idea, and those dealing with subject matter that cannot be perceived but only imagined. Euclid, an example of the first, treats of things by their nature perceptible that can be comprehended by anyone in any language, without knowledge of the author, his times, or the vicissitudes of his book. The true meaning of the Bible, an example of the second, is in many places inexplicable but only in reference to such matters as cannot be perceived clearly and distinctly. However, understood as a book solely dealing with moral questions the Bible is like Euclid and the reader may be sure of its true meaning. They are alike, argues Spinoza, because the precepts of true piety are universal, like the precepts of mathematics, and are expressed in very ordinary language. Other matters in the Bible that exceed questions of morality and true piety are curious, but they are not profitable, because they are not thought, or philosophy. In reference to Euclid no procedure or method of reading is required because one has (through the mind's own structures of understanding) direct access to his teaching. In reference to the Bible, however, a procedure is required, one that cuts through all the superfluity of the Bible and ferrets out only its clear and distinct, or universal ideas, that is, ideas already common to human understanding or unaided reason. In this respect the Bible is comparable to nature: it is confusing until its universal laws are understood. The interpretation of nature provides Spinoza with the rules for the proper interpretation of the Bible. Just as the interpretation of nature consists in examining the history of nature from which are deduced definitions of fixed axioms, so the proper interpretation of the Bible consists in examining its history and inferring the intention of its authors from its fundamental principles.

Spinoza states that the historical knowledge of Scripture consists of three parts: the nature and properties of the language in which the books were written, an arrangement of the contents of each book under appropriate heads, and the environment of all the books, or, in other words, the life and conduct of the author and the fate of the book. Inferring the intention of the authors from the fundamental principles of the Bible entails seeking first what is most universal and foundational to the Bible, that is, a doctrine commended by all biblical writers as eternal.

What one looks for when seeking a universal axiom is a sentence or phrase that is commonly used by a variety of different authors from a variety of times and places. By such a rule any idea that is only stated once must be considered unimportant. Thus the phrase 'Hear, O Israel, the Lord your God, the Lord is One' (which occurs only once, in Deut. 6:4) by Spinoza's reckoning is a biblical trifle, despite the fact that it is a fundamental notion to Judaism.

Subjects on which the Bible does not speak universally but which may be clear on rational grounds are not scriptural doctrine. From the universal doctrines flow less universal doctrines that nevertheless have regard to the general conduct of life. Certainty with regard to scriptural knowledge is not possible owing to the history and above all the ambiguity of the Hebrew language. However, matters that are founded in clear and distinct ideas cannot be obscured totally; moral questions, understood from universal doctrines, remain intelligible. True piety is not in jeopardy because the precepts of true piety are simple and easily understood. This method according to Spinoza requires only natural reason. It is a method critical of political theologians because it claims no need for a supernatural faculty, such as an indwelling of the Holy Spirit (Spinoza does not name but has in mind Calvin), or for a philosophical faculty, as advocated in the interpretive tradition of Maimonides.

Spinoza's procedures for interpreting the Bible, premising a view of nature antithetical to the traditional interpretation of the biblical account of creation, presuppose the Bible to be solely natural in origin. For it to have arisen from revelation would require a miracle, the action of God against nature. But God cannot have acted against that which is eternal and necessary. Natural in origin, and therefore interpreted according to the way of interpreting nature, the Bible cannot but be understood as complementing Spinoza's view of nature, i.e. the philosophical view.

In Spinoza's mind the method of interpreting nature is a model to be followed no matter what is to be interpreted. If what is to be interpreted does not readily yield to that method then the fault or problem lies in the thing interpreted, not in the method. In this case the Bible does not actually meet the expectations of the model, because that model presupposes a trustworthy history of the scriptural writings; however, the writers themselves and those who handed down the writings did not, he argues, preserve full historical information. The problem is compounded by the additions to and distortions of scripture by subsequent generations in the absence of correct historical information. The additions and distortions reflect theological prejudices that must be removed if scripture is to serve true piety, namely, obedience.

The chief prejudice, according to Spinoza, is that Moses composed the Pentateuch. Spinoza's conclusion regarding Moses' authorship follows from evidence that arises only once the prior assumption is made that the Bible has come to be naturally and only once the interpretation of the Pentateuch is set strictly within the principles of the interpretation of nature. By these principles the tradition of Moses' authorship becomes a 'prejudice' that conceals the true history of composition. The true history is concealed, argues Spinoza, because it exposes a natural, not a divinely guided, authorship, and a natural, not a divine, truth. This natural truth is accessible to reason insofar as it is universal. This universal truth has to do with obedience. There are no secret, metaphysical truths in the Pentateuch, no teachings destined only for the few.

In his well-known citing of Ibn Ezra as a predecessor to his own view, Spinoza is silent about what can be seen as Ibn Ezra's leading motive in his seemingly cryptic statements about Moses' authorship: to acknowledge in anticipation something similar to Spinoza's principles regarding the history of composition, but to articulate those principles in a way that preserves the view upheld or implied by the theory of Moses' authorship, namely, that the teachings of the Pentateuch are unified and that some of the teachings are mysterious. Such a position (that the Pentateuch is unified and profound) is explicit and articulate in Maimonides' *Guide to the Perplexed* and translates into a formidable theological teaching that runs counter to Spinoza's philosophic assumptions. That Maimonides is one of the very few thinkers whom Spinoza mentions by name suggests the high degree to which *TPT* is directed (a) against the monumental claim that the Pentateuch offers difficult teachings of a final character that refer directly to right conduct in human affairs and (b) against any specific tradition, such as Moses' authorship, that offers corollary support to that claim. Spinoza converts the theologico-political problem of authorship into a literary problem controlled by the principles for interpreting nature.

Because Spinoza has already established from his first argument that the Bible teaches only about morality and true piety, it follows that the actual historical fate and condition of the books will not detract from the central teaching of the books: to love God and neighbour. Insofar as the Bible contains doctrine, the doctrine is derivative of the central moral teaching. Spinoza allows that the doctrines indisputably depending on this teaching, and which are plainly taught by Scripture throughout, are that God exists, forsees all things, is Almighty, and causes the good to prosper and the wicked to suffer and that salvation depends on His grace. Such teachings as these, allowed by his method of interpretation, are innocuous to philosophy, because they are derivative not of the doctrine of creation but of the doctrine of obedience, which by the premise of his method cannot be seen as dependent on the doctrine of creation.

Spinoza's method of interpretation depends on his premise that the central teaching of Scripture is primarily a teaching that all men can know and understand and is thus solely a public teaching. Thus he must say that what the Scripture does contain by way of doctrine in the sphere of philosophy is simple and knowable to all men; the Bible contains nothing not known to reason, or nothing esoteric, knowable only to those who study it deeply. The precise intellectual knowledge of God is given only to the few philosophers; this is knowledge withheld from most men. But it is knowledge not necessary to their right actions. To argue this point Spinoza refers to the lives of Abraham and Moses. Abraham, who only knew God as El Sadai, did not thereby know the essence of God, but Abraham acted righteously. Moses who knew God as YHWH, did know the essence of God, but Moses complained to God and doubted his promises. Knowing God's justice and charity is sufficient for correct living, which, Spinoza insists, the Scripture everywhere plainly teaches.

THE THIRD ARGUMENT (CHAPTERS 16–20)

Spinoza's first two arguments remove from the Bible all doctrine contradictory to philosophy and posit as the central teaching of the Bible that men should live together in harmony. That they should live together harmoniously is taught above all (he argues in the third part of the treatise) by reason, which instructs men to overcome and transform the harsh reality of nature, or necessity, by submission to the common good. Biblical teaching properly understood (i.e. understood through Spinoza's biblical criticism) provides a revealed foundation to the political state properly understood and constituted by reason.

For Spinoza the proper foundation of the state rests not in man's knowing the proper way as taught by revelation, but in knowing wherein his self-interests lie. Spinoza's account of the state begins then with an account of nature, which by his prior assertion is necessary and eternal. From the standpoint of the Bible the right ordering of men is stated in Genesis 1 in terms of man's having dominion over the fish of the sea, over the fowl of the air, over the cattle, over all the earth, and over every moving thing that moves upon the earth; man is depicted as part of the whole, a seemingly pre-eminent part, with a directive to rule certain other parts of the whole, but not the whole itself. Man's rule is defined more particularly in Genesis 2 as serving and keeping what is given. This foundational biblical viewpoint is stated by way of marked contrast to Spinoza's arguing that the right ordering of men begins with a depiction of sovereignty in nature. 'Now it is the sovereign law and right of nature that each individual should endeavour to preserve itself as it is, without regard to anything but itself.'[23] Following through in detail the sequence and substance of Spi-

noza's third argument, relatively ignored by historians of biblical interpretation, unfolds the relation of his political philosophy to his biblical
criticism. The third argument has eight parts.

1 / Men in the state of nature have certain natural rights, among
them the right of self-preservation and the right to do whatever is
required by nature for the sake of self-preservation. Natural right is
determined by desire and power, not reason, and does not afford the
distinction between good and evil. Nevertheless, man's true good is
attained by living under the dictates of reason, not nature. Reason
teaches that men must for their highest good live together harmoniously, in a compact. A compact has as its end the greatest good and
least evil and it remains valid as long as it serves that end. A state is
formed by the willing transfer of all individual power or natural right
to the body politic which then comes to possess sovereign natural right
over all things. The body politic is a democracy, that is, a society that
wields all its power as a whole.

2 / In a democracy, Spinoza argues, there is no violation of individual
natural rights. Even in obeying the most absurd commandment of the
sovereign power, that right is retained inasmuch as duty in this respect
is a lesser evil and more directed toward self-preservation than toward
dissolution of the state. Furthermore, the sway of the tyrant is not long
retained unless it is directed toward the public good. From this foundation wherein natural rights are preserved in a society it follows that
civil right, like natural right, consists in the liberty to preserve one's
existence; wrong is any action contrary to sovereign power and disrup-
tive of the organized community; justice consists in rendering every
person his lawful due, and injustice in depriving a person of what the
law allows him. The state, not the Bible, not revelation, defines what is
right and wrong action.

3 / The state of nature is prior to the rise of religion. No man knows
to love his neighbour in the state of nature; but man learns to love his
neighbour through religion, the religion taught in the Bible. Likewise
through religion men agree to live in covenant and to relinquish their
natural rights, for the sake of mutual advantage. The rise of religion
and the rise of the civil state are coterminous, involving man's rational
decision. Religious law is not binding in any absolute sense; rather it

has validity only as it supports the civil state.[24] Inasmuch as the sovereign seeks to preserve the civil rights as well as the religious he should be obeyed in all things, even when he commands anything contrary to religion, unless, through an indisputable revelation of God's will, attested by a prophetic sign, the contrariness of his action is known.

4 / The foundation of the state is ideally said to consist in the transfer of individual natural rights to the body politic whose sovereignty may rest in one person or many, for every person retains some right in dependence on his own decision. However, the transfer of individual natural rights is itself an individual decision; obedience, no matter its motive, underlies submission to the sovereign. The sovereign offers concessions to subjects with a view to security and dominion so as to prompt obedience. The task and the goal of the sovereign are to frame institutions so that every man may prefer public right to private advantage. In Spinoza's view one chief worth of the Hebrew Bible is its record of the history of the Hebrew state with respect to Moses' success in enunciating public right and persuading the people to prefer it over private advantage.

5 / Spinoza reviews the history of the Hebrew nation to document its instructive character, arguing in effect that the Hebrew theocracy contained within it the model of democracy itself. On fleeing the Egyptians the Hebrews were bound by no covenant. Being then in the state of nature they transferred their rights to God. Their experience of his power ensured their preservation. Theirs was a theocracy in which civil authority and religious authority were the same. As in a democracy they all transferred equally their rights to God and had an equal right to consult God until such time as they transferred to Moses that right. The state remained theocratic even after Moses' death inasmuch as the seat of government was the Temple, because sole allegiance was to God, and because the general-in-chief was elected by God. All the laws that Moses promulgated had as their end inducing patriotism, which was the same as piety. The turning away from the law is to be explained as rebellion against the priests.

6 / Spinoza extracts four exemplary political doctrines from the history of the Hebrew commonwealth. It is hurtful to both religion and the state for ministers of religion to possess civil power. It is dangerous

for speculative matters to be relegated to ministers of religion. Decisions regarding right and wrong are best in the hands of the political sovereign. Democracy is superior to monarchy.

7 / The most exemplary political teaching follows from Spinoza's argument that religious law (including the precept to love one's neighbour and that same precept as derived from reason) attains the force of law solely from the sovereign inasmuch as law comes to be only when natural rights are surrendered to authority for the sake of the public good. It follows from this that outward observance of religion should be in accord with public peace as directed by the sovereign. By this conclusion Spinoza drives home his main theme and seals it by observing that the primary virtue of the Hebrew commonwealth was that the practice of religion depended entirely on the commands of the king.

8 / Spinoza would set limits upon the sovereign by distinguishing between action and thought. The commands of the sovereign refer to action proper for the peaceful state, not to religious beliefs or philosophical thoughts. On these matters the state has no authority except to guarantee that every citizen maintain the right to think and believe as is found pleasing to him. The peaceful state is best preserved if this right is upheld. In respect to this position Spinoza is the father of liberal democracy or the state based on the absolute tolerance of all views.

It can now be seen in what manner Spinoza's political philosophy necessitates his procedure for reading the Bible. The end that his political teaching seeks is freedom: in general, freedom for all men to think as they please, and, in particular, freedom for the philosopher to think without obstruction from either the magistrate or the sovereign. Such freedom presupposes a body politic in which all men agree to be obedient to the sovereign state in respect to all outward conduct, but in which men are allowed to think and believe at will. Inasmuch as the Bible has and will continue to influence men strongly,[25] the body politic must be educated into its proper use, because its improper use, namely as a source of metaphysical truths, leads to great dissension and controversy. Spinoza's procedure for reading the Bible would thus properly serve the masses by leading them to regard obedience as the Bible's central and sole teaching; his procedure would serve the potential philosopher by helping to create a body politic that tolerates differing thoughts and by releasing the potential philosopher from intellectual bondage to the Bible.

The relation of Spinoza's method of biblical interpretation to his political philosophy may now be concisely stated. His method serves as a mediator of his political philosophy to a two-fold audience, the potential philosophers and the masses. His method is a theological mediator in that it enables the potential philosopher to discern the non-historical teachings of the Bible in respect to the nature of things – the eternal truths about eternal things. The theological import of Spinoza's biblical criticism is to transform the potential philosopher into a philosopher by instructing him or her concerning the philosophical truths of the Bible. His method is a political mediator in that it enables the masses to discern the non-historical teachings of the Bible in respect to the right ordering of men. These teachings, summarized under the dictum that all men are to be obedient to sovereignty, while known to reason are well taught by the Bible because of its imaginative persuasiveness. The political import of Spinoza's biblical criticism is to transform the masses into obedient subjects of the civil magistrate.

III

This analysis of *TPT* has shown that Spinoza's account of the Bible is designed to fit his philosophical system and that his method of biblical interpretation, based in a prior critique that severely distinguishes between reason and revelation, attempts to mediate his metaphysics and its political corollary to the potential philosopher and to the masses. Attention is now given to clarifying in greater detail Spinoza's attempt to correlate his view of nature and his political thought by means of his historical investigations of the Bible.[26]

Set out as the way to determine the truth of the Bible, Spinoza's method of interpretation stands explicitly in opposition to the theory of verbal inspiration held by Calvin and to the interpretive synthesis of philosophy and theology worked out by Maimonides. Spinoza does not take the final step of declaring biblical revelation dispensable as an independent source of knowledge, but his critique and its methodological unfolding do reduce the content of revelation to its moral teaching (i.e. obedience to God, justice, and charity) and disputes authority granted to the Bible as a source of secure theological doctrine. Thus isolated and removed from its original context, the ethical content of the Bible is woven into the fabric of Spinoza's 'natural' religion. Spinoza's 'natural' religion is an important component in his political doctrine because it operates as an ideological support for the democratic order: biblical religion persuades the masses to acknowledge their duty of obedience to the political authority as a divine sanction. In this way the ethical content of the Bible is pressed into the service of the democratic state; obedience to God is moulded into obedience to the sovereign magistrate.

Moreover, according to Spinoza, ecclesiastical or theological spokesmen have no legitimate protest in this matter, for the Bible offers no really contradictory doctrine about the best ordering of men. Because it is made historically relative as a source of clear and definite teaching concerning the best ordering of men, the Bible is neutralized as a source of serious opposition to political philosophy. In fact Spinoza turns the history related therein to his own advantage, as a means to illustrate the truth of his political doctrine. The Bible is useful as a supportive document because of its imaginative and traditional appeal to the populace.

Although he exploits the appeal of the Bible to the 'masses,' there can be no doubt that for Spinoza the idea of the historicity of the Bible is essentially a negative feature. Knowledge conveyed through the appeal to imagination has neither the certainty nor the strength of truth associated with reasoned insight and clear and distinct ideas. On the basis of his understanding of human nature and natural right, Spinoza can conclude only that the contractual order of rationalized self-interest is vulnerable to the play of passion and imagination that characterizes the life of most men. In this regard his effort to enlist biblical support for his political doctrine is a resigned concession to the harsh fact that the masses cannot be won over solely by reason. Spinoza's method of historical investigation is not meant to serve as a philosophical justification of biblical teaching; on the contrary, it is intended to promote insight into the limits of religious certainty, which is founded upon theoretical doctrines taught in traditional biblical and political theology. Indeed, his historical investigations serve as a demonstration that the Bible teaches no doctrines upon which any certainty in thought can be founded.

Spinoza's basically negative assessment of the historical knowledge communicated in the Bible raises an intriguing question: despite the hostile reception of Spinoza's treatise among the orthodox, how did it happen that his historical criticism eventually developed and was consolidated within orthodox circles? To put the question more directly, how did it happen that Spinoza's call for historical criticism of the Bible increasingly became a demand for it.

The answer to this question lies beyond the scope of this paper and demands a complete study in itself, which remains to be conducted.[27] However, the central issue of such a study may be concisely stated here.

The political corollary to Spinoza's view of the eternality of nature is Spinoza's democracy, which is the agreement of men to turn over their natural rights (which allow no distinction between good and evil in respect to self-preservation) to a sovereign power in return for its protection. In this democracy freedom is limited to freedom of thought because in fact all actions are restrained by obedience to the sovereign. The restraint upon freedom of action is but the political expression of Spinoza's view of the eternality and necessity of nature, in which all things necessarily, not freely, exist. This view is antithetical to the view that things exist freely, that things came to exist by a choice and that they thus have a history that is wrought by choices. From the standpoint of the Bible things have come to be by God's choice to create them and have a history wrought by choice: for example, according to Genesis 3 man had a choice between dying and living forever, but chose death. Within this view of the historicity of creation as distinct from the eternality of nature there can be no teaching that is eternally true; there are only historical truths that come to be and pass away. The teachings of the Bible are themselves historical. Indeed, by Spinoza's own historical investigations the teachings of the Bible regarding the right ordering of men, that is, the laws, are shown to be historically rather than eternally true. The political corollary of the biblical view of the historicity of creation is theocracy, which is the agreement of men to be instructed and governed by God. Spinoza opposes theocracy by democracy because he opposes the doctrine of creation by the doctrine of eternal necessity. His mode of opposing the biblical account of creation and theocracy, or the rule by God, is by the method of the historical investigation of the Bible. By these investigations Spinoza exposes all that is uncertain, or only historically true, and uncovers the residue of eternally true teachings.

A study that would properly understand the imperative demand in Spinoza's founding of biblical criticism would thus see that the intent of Spinoza's historical criticism of the Bible is to undermine the most obvious and primary teaching of the Bible, namely the historicity of creation. By discovering the historicity of the composition and transmission of the Bible and from this discovery concluding that what the Bible teaches was true only once and in regard to the times in which it was written, Spinoza turns men inevitably to philosophy for guidance. But such historical investigations as Spinoza initiated derive their power precisely from the biblical teaching about the historicity of the whole. Attention to the history of biblical teaching, in the form of the historico-critical examination of its books, follows rightly from the teaching that men understand themselves and their ordering not *sub specie aeternitatis*, but by 'beginnings' (Gen. 1:1) and 'generations' (Gen. 2:4). But such exclusive attention to the history of the Bible falls far short of fully respecting the integrity and wholeness of biblical thought. Such a study of the Bible surrenders to Spinoza's negative assessment of the biblical account of history because such a study no longer seeks to understand and explicate the political corollary to the view of the historicity of nature.

By focusing on his negative view of history, if not his anti-historical motive, the careful reader of Spinoza sees more clearly the relation of Spinoza's doctrine of eternal necessity and its political corollary to his historical critique of the Bible. Seeing this relation, one will understand that Spinoza's biblical criticism does not finally serve to neutralize the Bible for the sake of freedom, because creatures rightly understood by the doctrine of eternal necessity have no freedom. Spinoza's biblical criticism rather serves to conceal the account of history in the Bible such that it can no longer be seen as teaching historicity. The historico-

critical examination of the Bible, under the dictates of Spinoza's procedures, is a quest for necessary truths available to reason, not the truths
the Bible is at pains to teach are available by revelation.

The science of biblical interpretation that has come to be since
Spinoza is one that has increasingly focused on the problems raised by
Spinoza in his second argument (chapters 7–15). In so doing it has
given over to theologians and philosophers the problems raised by Spi-
noza in his first argument (chapters 1–6), and to political scientists and
theoreticians the problems raised in his third argument (chapters 16–20).
To honour Spinoza, contemporary biblical scientists would recall that
Spinoza fathered biblical criticism in order to found liberal democracy,
and in such recollection ponder anew what the Bible, in particular the
Pentateuch, teaches to be the right, or the good, political order.[28]

NOTES

1 Robert Pfeiffer *Introduction to the Old Testament* (New York: Harper Brothers
   1948) 46

2 Leo Strauss *Spinoza's Critique of Religion* (New York: Schocken 1965) 16

3 R.H.M. Elwes *The Chief Works of Benedict de Spinoza* (New York: Dover 1951)

4 Cheyne *Founders of Old Testament Criticism* (London: Methuen 1893) makes a
   passing reference to 'the lonely Jewish thinker of Amsterdam' (12), but solely as a
   critic of the Pentateuch. J. Coppens *The Old Testament and the Critics* (New
   Jersey: St. Anthony Press 1942) cites Spinoza as a deistic philosopher but only in
   the context of advocating without question the superiority of 'the critico-historical
   method' (7). Emil Kraeling *The Old Testament since the Reformation* (New York:
   Harper 1955) regards Spinoza as 'the precursor of the great critical movement' (45)
   by reference to Spinoza's assertions about the Pentateuch and fails to note the
   impact of Spinoza's philosophy upon those very assertions. Kraus *Geschichte der
   historisch – kritischen Erforschung des AT* (Neukirchener Verlag 1956) cites
   Spinoza in connection with 'die literarhistorische Problematik in der alltestamentli-
   chen Forschung' but does not relate those insights to Spinoza's larger philosophical
   enterprise.

5 See, for example, A.G. Wernham *Benedict de Spinoza: The Political Works* (Oxford:
   Clarendon 1958). In giving the text and translation of *TPT*, Wernham deletes
   chapters 7–13, which are the chapters Spinoza devotes to his biblical criticism.

6 In his preface, Spinoza claims to have 'constructed a method of Scriptural interpretation' (*TPT* 8). Throughout this essay the phrase 'biblical methodology' or 'biblical criticism' is used as an abbreviation of Spinoza's longer phrase.

7 For the overall lines of this section, see Leo Strauss *What Is Political Philosophy?* (Glencoe, Ill: Free Press 1959) and in particular the first essay, 'What Is Political Philosophy?,' 9–55.

8 Ibid 11

9 Ibid 12

10 Ibid 12

11 See Leo Strauss *Natural Right and History* (Chicago: University of Chicago Press 1953) 165–251.

12 On the relation of Spinoza to Machiavelli, see Leo Strauss *Spinoza's Critique of Religion* (New York: Schocken 1965) 224–50. On the relation between Hobbes and Spinoza, see Wernham *Spinoza* 12ff.

13 *TPT* concerns the whole Bible, i.e. the Christian Bible, including the New Testament. Nevertheless, the primary object of Spinoza's critique is the Old Testament, or the Jewish Bible, and in particular the first five books, the Pentateuch. To analyse carefully his thinking about the teachings of the New Testament is beyond the scope of this essay. Strauss's partial treatment of this matter is very illuminating. See 'How to Study Spinoza's *Theologico-Political Treatise*' in *Persecution and the Art of Writing* (Westport, Conn: Greenwood 1973) 142–201, especially 171ff. That the *TPT* concerns especially the Pentateuch is evidenced by the attention Spinoza devotes to Moses, the traditional author of the Pentateuch, in chapters 1–6 and 17.

14 For example, these are the only chapters noted by Pfeiffer *Introduction*.

15 *TPT* 25

16 See Strauss 'How to Study' 184ff.

17 *TPT* 11

18 On the importance of the biblical account of creation, and Spinoza's concealed attention to it, see Strauss, 'How to Study' 199–200.

19 That this view is an oversimplified statement about the account of creation in Genesis 1 should be recognized. The text speaks only of *creatio ex nihilo* by implication, although it speaks explicitly of the pre-existence of the 'waste and void.' The point may be registered here that Spinoza's strategy in dealing with the Bible is to state as *the* teaching of the Bible the oversimplified, if not simplistic, teaching known in popular thinking.

20 *TPT* 40

21 Ibid 99
22 Ibid. In not allowing 'theological prejudices' to enter biblical interpretations, Spinoza does not caution against the philosophical presuppositions that govern his analysis of biblical teaching in the first section of *TPT*.
23 Ibid 200
24 One has to remember that by 'religious law' Spinoza has in mind what he calls 'ceremonial law' as distinct from 'divine (= natural) law' (ibid 57ff).
25 In his preface Spinoza argues that men are at all times superstitious and that they always prefer the prophet over the philosopher, or imagination over thought. In his analysis, the Bible is the product of imagination, not thought. For this reason, it will always influence men (ibid 3–4).
26 I wish to thank Mr James Robinson, a former graduate student, for helping me think through and compose some points concerning the relation of Spinoza's view of nature to his historical investigations of the Bible.
27 The background to an answer is provided by Ernst Cassirer *The Philosophy of the Enlightenment* (Princeton: Princeton University Press 1951) 182ff.
28 How little current biblical scholarship sees its current task to entail a recovery of the theologico-political issues in *TPT* is illustrated by Peter Stuhlmacher's discussion of 'a way out of the dilemma' in *Historical Criticism and Theological Interpretation Scripture* (Philadelphia: Fortress 1977) 76ff.

JAMES DOULL

Naturalistic individualism: Quebec independence and an independent Canada

I

The question that has long agitated Canadians, whether Quebec will remain part of the confederation and what revisions of the constitution may be necessary to satisfy this and other particular interests, is obscured by the current language of political discussion. George Grant, for example, some years back in his *Lament for a Nation*, showed that Canadian independence was already lost, that Canada was to be regarded as part of the American economic empire. What has been lost is that particular relation of belief and culture to the practical and political realm that we received from a British and continental European tradition. When it is argued that the Québécois must be independent in order to save their language and culture, that sounds strange if they, with other Canadians, already live in a culture set adrift from economic and political life. Among English Canadians much is said about the danger to our culture from American influences, yet they live and work in a technological culture whose influence they deplore.

The *indépendantistes* of Quebec do not, any more than English Canadians, propose to isolate themselves from the affluent North American economy. They do not desire an independent French state in an older sense of political sovereignty, but rather to live more naturally in their own language in the technological empire – and participate more within their province in the management of it. From their culture and belief they are in revolt and, like English Canadians, have an interest only in saving what has lost truth and authority for them and is for them an unreal subjective realm as against the economic and technological.

In the older culture from which Canadians received their institutions it was not assumed that the economic realm had this priority but that it was subservient to the state and, in other ways, to the family and the church. The subordination of economic life to other objective ends may frequently have been ineffective or at the price of diverse oppressions. That it should be possible was secured by a subordination of the economic class to those of a less confined and technical interest, among whom kings and aristocrats, clergy, artists, and learned and wise men had their several parts to play. The helplessness now generally felt among the more cultivated about any reasonable control and direction of the great technological economy is foreign alike to the older Christian tradition and to its classical antecedents. One may say that technology is a modern phenomenon and far different from the arts of an older time and the distribution of their products. The difference is not, however, so much in technology as in an altered assumption about what is real and primary. It is not thought that the objective authority of institutions that might control economic life is compatible with individual freedom. The individual has made himself the measure of the former objective order and has then discovered that he is at the mercy of economic forces from which he has only an abstract and inner freedom.

The revolution by which those of a European and Christian tradition have passed from objective and rational institutions to a free naturalistic individuality is not new; it has been happening in some ways and some places for a century and a half. Yet English-speaking peoples have not yet adapted old habits of thought to the new freedom. The change has come upon them less noticeably and without the violence in which the old order was destroyed elsewhere. But the same revolution has occurred and had already taken place in principle when one began to detach an English tradition – with or without a revolutionary American adjunct – from the common classical and Christian world of Europeans. Then a primacy began to be given to natural differences, of which nationalism is one form, and the anarchic individualism of the present time. The monarchy and parliamentary government continued in Britain and the colonial peoples of British descent. One spoke as though monarchy, lords, and commons were the elements of the constitution while at the same time individuals thought themselves more and more the source of authority, and power passed from the state to economic society. Philosophically the empirical tradition of Locke and Hume might appear to continue, or one might oppose to it continental borrow-- ings, but the linguistic philosophy of recent times obviously takes much better account of the total shift from the universal to the natural and particular.

There is not likely a great difference between English and French Canadians in their relation to the naturalistic individualism now commonly assumed as the basis of the state and other institutions. The difference is in the various content they give to this principle. While the content has ceased to be authoritative and one's relation to it has ceased to be serious, one is attached to the linguistic and other natural expressions of a vanishing order. Between these particularities there is no discourse. For there is not a common tradition unless it be the abstract technological reason that is the other element of this naturalistic individualism. But it is from that abstract reason that one flees to the particularity one feels to belong to oneself as Québécois, Ontarian, Acadian, Nova Scotian, or whatever. The difficulty in finding appropriate constitutional arrangements for all Canadians arises from mistaking the nature of these particularities. It is possible to insist on them as though they were to have other reality than linguistic, aesthetic, or customary. Independence might mean political sovereignty in the old sense, when no more was intended or desired than that people should be able to protect themselves in their own particular way against the devastating uniformity of technological society.

Only in secondary ways is the question of political unity in Canada peculiar. In Britain old national differences in Wales and Scotland assume a certain political importance as people are repelled from the economic society and its conservative or socialist politicians. The concreteness of life the old institutions gave is sought by individuals in what is near and felt, traditions as visible, heard, performed. At the same time as the national state has become dependent on the European Economic Community and multinational technology to maintain individuals in their natural freedom, they take flight from the abstractness of life to diverse particularities. Whether in western Europe, in the

United States, or in the Soviet Union and its satellites there is in general the same collapse of an objective religious belief and of secular institutions grounded in that belief. There are differences of great importance in the old order and the manner of its transition to individualistic naturalism – whether this revolution was more intrinsic or imposed from without and in the stage the new individualism has reached in its development. For the present argument these differences will be largely ignored. The question will be of the nature and origin of this naturalistic individualism, its political and religious implications, and the beginnings of its collapse. It is only possible to speak clearly about the particular Canadian form of natural liberation to the extent that the general concept has been elucidated.

II

It is said of the supposed right of the French in Quebec to self-determination that the age of independent nations is past. At the conquest of Quebec in 1759 it had not yet begun. When now the Québécois appeal to such a right they are indeed assuming that what we have now in Canada is the maturity of the Victorian state of the 1867 confederation, whereas the English and French nations have outgrown their colonial and European dependence and now will go naturally their own ways. In such a view it would be no more reasonable to persist in a federal state than to suppose the French and English peoples in Europe could have federated in the nineteenth century.

The argument that national states and their right to self-determination are anachronistic rests on the observation that western Europe itself – where the national state originated and flourished – has gone over to an economic association that tends toward a political federation, and that in the Soviet Union and its neighbours and in North America multinational economic states are now the prevailing political form. Nationalism and the national states of the nineteenth century are the beginning of a reversion to nature from the intellectuality of classical and Christian thought. The economic empires that have succeeded them are a further return to nature and have their principle in a deeper revolt against the rationality of that tradition. Not the national community but the economic independence of its individual members is thought to be basic in this newer naturalism.

Both nationalism and the economic individualism of the present time are to be understood as stages in the decline of Europe and of the American extensions of its culture – a decline that has some parallels with the decline of the free states of classical antiquity. There individuals in the course of time freed themselves from an objective system of rights and duties and came to regard themselves in their private interests as the elements of the state and other institutions. With this individualization of life government ceased to be in any effective way the affair of the people and assumed rather the form of despotic and bureaucratic power.

The history of free institutions is altogether different in Christian times than in classical antiquity. In the theology of the western church a stronger break was made with Greek thought (while all the same retaining it at a level far above the superficial theologies of the present time which oppose Judaic to Hellenic, Moses to Aristotle) with the knowledge that freedom is to be found not in nature but in thought. The natural in its opposition to the rational is evil and not as it should be. On the uncompromising Augustinian destruction of every natural beginning could begin the discovery of an order in which the natural was regarded as derivative or created and not prior to and independent of thought. Into this intellectual attitude were drawn the barbarous tribes who succeeded to the western Empire in their religious belief and by degrees in their secular institutions. If the church was for long the primary society – the only sovereign state in a strict sense – this direct authority waned as kings made their rule effective over the estates. In the absolute authority of Renaissance kings one sees the natural and, in a Christian view, evil will of feudal lords and townsmen subordinated to the rational. The basis then exists on which the estates can reassert their place in the realm but as mutually limited and without the endless disorder of feudalism.

The peculiar character of the European culture of the older modern period restored nature on the basis of its negation, not abstractedly but according to the concreteness of Christian belief, so far as this was able to be expressed in the state and other institutions as well as in freer contemplative forms. In this sense there might be said to be a return to nature, but the original Augustinian aversion to nature remained presupposed and the natural was built into the rational and universal as its principle.

The beginning of the decline of this Christian European culture cannot be better described than by Marx when he speaks of an end to the alienation of the individual from nature and the return to a natural immediacy – to a community of natural individuals. The long correction and education of humanity in Christian times, so that at length a harmony and concretion of nature and thought comes into view, appears as an immediate result. The state is to be absorbed into civil society and made the servant of the natural will. Family and church are forms of suppression. The economy is to be taken in hand and made to serve free natural individuals.

The revolution Marx speaks of was general and in no way simply the work of those called Marxists. Indeed the conspiratorial revolutionaries who bring natural freedom to Africans, who have never known anything else, to China, or wherever do another work than they suppose. They bring subjective freedom to where it has no roots and must be far more destructive of life than were the merchants and missionaries of the previous century. The truer Marxism is the technological society of United States and the European Economic Community. For here the natural liberation of individuals – the common end of these and of the Soviet society – is not so directly and brutally contradicted by the bureaucratic apparatus as it is in Soviet society. That industry is in some sense privately owned and controlled in this Western socialism is a secondary consideration. A less direct government regulation of the economy in these countries permits more easily the coexistence of anarchic socialism and bureaucratic socialism, which in more imperfect and abstract forms of Marxism are found to be incompatible.

It conflicts, no doubt, with the usual language of the social scientists to call the United States a socialist and even Marxist society. There remained until recently not a little of the original eighteenth-century enlightened capitalist ethos about the American people. But from the abstract rationality of an older capitalism and their Puritan origins Americans have been liberated by a half-century of Freud and such influences. Only the Vietnam war, and the conflict it disclosed between the new natural freedom and the old order, was necessary to complete the revolution. There is now nothing natural or unnatural in the soul that is not thought to have its right. Natural right in this sense is limited only by the other aspect of this freedom, which is an equality to be applied without restriction to all humanity – and indeed, as appears to some, to whales, seals, and whatever creature may be so favoured.

Between the equalizing tendency of this freedom and the endless difference and inequality of natural – and unnatural – desires there is a conflict which social scientists would resolve in diverse ways. It being assumed that the origin of just government is the will of liberated individuals, there is a question how far and in what form they should contract to give authority to state bureaucracies and other corporations or institutions. There revive here in a way the old controversies of political philosophy about the social contract. But there is need to attend to a fundamental difference: in the older argument the natural was not thought to have any right as such, but only so far as founded on the rational will. In the natural or socialist – neo-liberal – freedom, not the rational is made the basis of right but nature itself. What is to be feared in rulers, according to this view, is not the irrational and arbitrary violence that Locke or the American constitution sought to guard against, but rather reason itself or the universal, as repressive of natural differences. The relation of rulers and ruled is therefore to be spoken of in a Marxist language of anarchy, bureaucracy, direct democracy, and the like, which avoids the profounder division of rational and natural common in one way or another to all forms of the older political philosophy, be they Lockean, Utilitarian, or whatever.

The reversion to nature in its primary form retains the confidence which it owes to its Christian antecedents that nature is amenable to human ends. There is both a return to the primitive – to the original Paradise one might say – and through technology one is beyond the alienation of all previous history. Technology is neither science nor the capitalist economy socialists write about, but rather both together as they serve liberated, natural individuals. The difference is obvious if one considers that the older capitalism, the bourgeois culture of, for example, the American or the French revolution, promised freedom to the enlightened, to the reasonable. To the socialist there is in this reason the extreme point of alienation. What he offers in its place is freedom in the natural and bodily and a reason that should not be abstracted and made an end above individuals free in their bodies.

What free individuals agree to recognize in common as natural and in what order may vary widely. Race and language may appear the basis of their association, and then one has what is called Fascism or Nazism after certain notorious examples. One may instead regard as first the common necessities of physical life, and the association that should serve these ends as prior to national differences is called socialism, communism, liberalism. These forms, often thought to be greatly opposed, one should rather see as having a common principle. They have all lost the consciousness of evil and responsibility, especially as these are found among Christians, in that they are no longer alienated but assume themselves to be immediately justified in their natural will. Evil no longer means a disharmony of nature and reason, to be corrected so far as may be by the discipline of secular and sacred institutions, but is the accidental failure of technology and its agents. Much is written about the Hitlers and Stalins and the organized evil of the twentieth century, but usually by those who in some part share its principle. Not the return to nature and an invincible confidence in the immediate goodness of the natural will is given as the cause, but rather vestiges of an unliberated reason. Thus socialists always call their enemies revisionists, and conservatism and such words serve the same purpose for neo-liberals. In this they touch only the surface of the evil and are ignorant that the direct, unmediated assertion of the natural against the rational is the total evil figured in the tradition by the devil.

Nothing is perhaps more characteristic of the new natural freedom, which takes as its immediate possession the long historical mediation of reason and nature in Christian and pre-Christian times, than, in the internal government of states, the computer, and, in relations among states, the nuclear bomb. In both, one has the extreme of abstract and externalized reason. Since the natural will of individuals is presupposed to be good and not to be corrected by reason and the authority of rational institutions, the demand is made on government to take account of a limitless variety of group and individual interests. In place of an internal adaptation of this proliferation of interests by education and the cultivation of a rational and responsible will, which would be regarded as evil and a violation of nature, the determination is made externally by the abstract and unassailable authority of the computer. The bomb is similarly the evil and competitive will of nations put from them as a thing, whereby they can enjoy the conviction that they are peace-loving people and war an accident or due to revisionist, that is rational, tendencies on the part of their opponents. In truth the natural will in its immediacy is sheer competitiveness, expansive without internal limit.

Thus considered, natural freedom appears quite the opposite of itself – as rather a condition in which the regulation of the natural has passed to a formal and contentless reason. One would give recognition and equality to whatever is in the will: because it exists it is good. The equalization of all differences is, however, their destruction as immediate, and the will of individuals turns out to be abstract, arbitrary, contentless. This contradiction of natural freedom in itself is overlooked, however, because it begins as the assurance that it is the fulfilment of all past forms, that it has made its own the concreteness of the Christian principle. One has thus in the decadence of Europe and America an unheard-of knowledge of history – of the arts, religions, external history of former times – and all this information available on demand from computerized libraries! The arts as well are productive as never before; new religions and philosophies grow up like mushrooms. The human spirit seems to itself rich when in truth it is empty and impoverished. For the past is not studied as educative and corrective, but as what one is already done with and liberated from. It is the object of an abstract and superficial reason that can without trouble rise above whatever content: and the arts and other works of the present endlessly repeat the same tale that between reason and the endlessness of the natural there is no congruity and true expression. There is a sharing and communication of experience in which nothing is in truth shared or communicated, since that would be a true object and an offence thus to freedom.

The relation of liberated moderns to the past is also nostalgic. Such moderns would not only be beyond all past forms but also at the same time desire them – would be subject to rational institutions, have a religion but not the religiosity that studies religion from beyond, etc. There is formed thus a conservative attitude within the principle of free, natural individuality. Of this conservative tendency there are innumerable appearances. Peculiarly striking, because they touch the principle so nearly, are the conflicts about abortion on demand and respect for life, the efforts of private groups to save the whale, the seal, Eskimos, and other primitive peoples. In such examples appears the contradiction already noticed of the principle itself. For it is not proposed, either in these or in cases where the separation of the natural from the abstract and technological is less simple, that natural freedom should subordinate itself to the universal. The natural is not to be grounded in law and authoritative institutions, which would appear inhuman and against natural right. The protests and demonstrations to save nature and the environment lack all seriousness; one holds to the natural against the technological reason by which one is free in it – and is not willing to give up anything of this freedom.

What is described is the first stage in the decadence of European freedom. The authority of old institutions and a concrete rational freedom did not of course give way quickly, but one lived for long between the old and the new. It might be assumed that the state and other institutions were there to serve the interests of individuals and not to educate them to rationality, while monarchy, church, family continued to exercise something of their traditional authority. The inertia of rational institutions, once established, is great and persistent even when liberated individuals have lost all understanding of them and, consistently with their principle, would demolish them. The chief point is that the classes have in principle been integrated into the state; all will in the course of time have equal political rights. So far as this equality is taken as immediate, and everyone feels himself free *qua* Englishman or whatever, a conflict sets in between this freedom and its mediation through the classes and great institutions – between felt freedom and law in the comprehensive sense of the ethical or institutional order. The conflict occurs for the reason already given, that between the sense of free individuality and the division of life in economic society or the system of means to a free life there is an endless discrepancy: the means are ever insufficient, one must await a greater perfection of technology; meanwhile one is subject to the discipline and dividedness of specialized labour – a discipline that seems without justice since one is conscious of being already a free individual.

With this conflict occurs the second stage in the decadence of European (and American) life. If the great theorist of the first stage is perhaps Marx, that of the second is Nietzsche. For through Nietzsche an attitude and a way of thinking of older origin have made themselves prevalent in the course of the present century. In place of the older order one had come to assume in the later nineteenth century a naturalism and against it an abstract moralistic idealism. Marx and the socialists would draw these elements into one view: the free natural individuality they proposed combined these elements. Such is in general the technological culture of the present time. In the United States, where it occurs in its purest and simplest form, it is commonly assumed that technology and a free naturalistic individuality can sustain each other. Against this socialism Nietzsche protested that it is rather the destruction and enslavement of free individuals.

This protest is of the utmost importance. For in the first or socialist decadence was contained in a diminished form the Christian belief that an agreement and a concrete unity of reason and nature were possible and were true humanity. Though it might assume atheistic forms, as with Marx, it could as well appear as a nature Christianity – its fulfilment particularly as against the inwardness of Protestant belief. Certain forms of a return to older Catholicism were no great distance from this free naturalism and might indeed be thought to be its religion. To more careful students of theology this immediate and natural concreteness, whether in secular or religious form, must seem doubtfully Christian. Interest has passed, still more strongly than in pietistic and other subjective forms of the eighteenth century, from the universal and true to individual feeling and opinion – unless in the felt objectivity of ritual and symbol. It is not hard for the theologian to applaud Nietzsche's animus against what he took for Christianity and the dessicating, despiritualizing power of economic society. In both was already assumed as principle an immediate natural individuality. Nietzsche's criticism points to the discrepancy between this assumption and its negation in a moralistic liberal or socialist society. With Nietzsche is effected a division of the elements the free natural individual would combine in economic society. In a modern way of speaking, he shows that technology and natural freedom are incapable of being combined – that their unity is a nihilistic will in which nature is not fulfilled, as assumed, but destroyed.

But in Nietzsche is found the curious belief of socialists and neo-liberals that they bring not a decadence and rejection but a completion of the European tradition. Both groups delight to think themselves good Europeans. So completely have they lost a sense of the negativity and untruth of the immediate natural, on which sense was built the European tradition, that they do not know their thought as rather a forgetting of that tradition and of the strong rationality of Greek and Roman antiquity. If it is understandable how the socialist or neo-liberal naturalism, which would hold in unbroken unity the primitive – the original Paradise – and the most sophisticated reason, could be taken for Christian by theologians, it is more wonderful that Nietzsche and Heidegger, his great interpreter, can appear as supplying a logical basis of Christian belief. The explanation is no doubt that in the decadence of Christian Europe there remains a desire for the concrete – an assumption that the true is that in which nature and reason are united. When this concreteness is not present in the technological naturalism of the socialist or neo-liberal, one looks for it in the anti-technological naturalism of Nietzsche and Heidegger. But there the rational has been attenuated to the extreme, out of care for the natural. Of the concrete rationality of European thought and the Christian religion only a shadow remains. But this to the theologians is no doubt a better foundation than none at all.

The decadence of the European principle is that one thinks to have hold of it immediately or naturally. That the principle is lost in this immediacy and that there is no natural freedom, such as is sought, are recognized slowly and with difficulty. While this discovery is taking place it is unclear whether there has been decline or progress, freedom or the loss of it. Nietzsche celebrates a pagan Germanic freedom. So far as his thought is in opposition to technological reason he might be expected to stay with this barbarous natural will, much as in our time one looks nostalgically to the primitive in one form or other, would have part in it, and would protect its survivals from the encroachments of technology. The interest of his position is that he does not remain in this opposition but gives a rational foundation or principle to the primitive or barbarous will. In this way he separates the natural from the rational and subjective aspect of technological freedom. His principle is a Being or Becoming logically anterior to the division of an abstract subjectivity from its content and in general to the being of beings or all the finite.

The philosophical defence and exposition of this position were especially the work of Heidegger. There is need, it is argued, that we return to the beginnings of European thought among the pre-Socratic philosophers, and understand the departure from the beginning as at every stage a farther entanglement in finite thought and loss of knowledge of Being. This is indeed a true and necessary argument if one begins, as Nietzsche did, with the return to nature and observes that the technical, moral society of the nineteenth century – as still more our advanced technology – is destructive of natural freedom and cannot be made its servant. The reason that will let the natural be and not expose it to the devastation of an endless, insatiable technology must be that in which the finite and, above all, modern subjectivity has not grounded itself and found its justification. The accurate theologian will say that it is the first and most abstract thought that thus leaves the natural untouched, that by its measure one will rightly think with Parmenides that all the finite is simple nullity. But if it is presupposed, as where Nietzsche takes up the argument, that the true and concrete are the natural, it is rightly said that this Being is its principle.

The excellence of this Nietzschean or Heideggerian philosophy is that it does away with its own naturalistic assumption. In it are the true criticism and destruction of technological naturalism or the incomplete decadence, as it was called. For it has the same presupposition as this and brings to light what is in it, namely a principle according to which the natural is nothing. But in the historical context of the argument there is much difficulty in accepting this simple conclusion. Both the technological and the anti-technological naturalism stand in relation to the European and Christian tradition. Natural rights are not, one may say, natural, that is immediate, but are the demand made on nature by a Christian tradition that has forgotten its mediation and the difficulty with which truth was found in the natural. It is no longer in thought and a rational belief that Europeans and Americans have their essential tradition, but in the natural and particular. One speaks, for example, of British, German, or some other national philosophy, as though national differences divided essentially and did not only dispose to the discovery of one rather than another principle. It is to the local, regional, and national that one is attached. The church once was common to Europeans or divided them into a small number of partial churches most of which respected the same ancient doctrine. Now the universal church is the abstraction of ecumenical discussions, and the real church is indefinitely particularized locally and temporally, as though into a multiplicity of pagan cults. A medieval church in reverse one might say: then the universal was known as primary, and the animation of the particularities. And so in other realms. That there is in this new view a desire to conserve the tradition in its manifold content and variety is conspicuous. But it is an effort to conserve the derivative and give it primacy, because there is no longer capacity for the thought and concrete universality that is the origin of this various content.

This weakening of the universal appears in the disintegration of institutions, most conspicuously perhaps in the United States where old forms have less of historical continuity. The family is absorbed into the individualism of economic society. And the Nietzschean or anti-technological naturalism cannot arrest the decay. For the cause is not the abstract, technological will merely, but the naturalistic assumption common to both positions. For the family of the Christian and European tradition is a rational institution and has its foundation in the universal. In the state, likewise the decline of government into technological bureaucracy is unaffected by nostalgic attachment to the monarchy and the preservation of venerable ceremonies. For the European state was founded not on nature but on the renunciation of it and cannot be renovated so long as one supposes free natural individuals to be its basis.

The anti-technological naturalism of Nietzsche and Heidegger attracts and is greatly influential in part because it appears to protect this cultural and religious particularity against an abstract, dissolving reason. Its true importance, as indicated, is quite the opposite of this: nothing whatever of all these cultural and religious particularities is sustained by this philosophy. It invites and requires one to look beyond the limits of that tradition and 'go pagan.' There is great indirect advantage for Christians and Europeans if they follow the argument to that conclusion. For in it appears an end to the natural or immediate Christianity which is the principle of socialist and neo-liberal technology. It is repugnant no doubt to the cultural arrogance of Europeans and to the exclusiveness of Christians to go to school again with the pagans, and not with Aristotle but with the first Greek philosophers and even Indian gymnosophists. Love of paganism, the more primitive the better, is indeed found everywhere – but merely as the movement from reason to nature. It is another matter at the end of that liberation to learn from the pagans that there are no natural rights – that there is no right except so far as the natural has been grounded in reason. The knowledge that this is so is older than Christianity. It is presupposed in the Christian and European tradition and, when forgotten, can be relearned from the pagans.

III

Technological naturalism is destructive of the natural because it would equalize all differences and give them the form of abstract subjectivity. Evil appears to be an excess of rationality, the inheritance of a Christian and European past. Would it not be better instead to live in nature aesthetically, as has been the character of the great cultures of the Far East – the Chinese and Japanese? The love of the primitive and, were it but humanly possible, of sheer animality, to which one strives in technological naturalism, is abandoned. It was sought in the other liberation because there was to be realized secularly the concrete unity of natural and rational of Christian belief – toward which end there could not well be an excess of animality. Here instead the natural is limited in relation to a principle. It is not to be equated with the principle, but rather the difference of natural beings from the principle is to be respected, as is the difference also respected of the thinking and practical relation of humans to natural beings and their knowledge of the principle. In this distance from the principle it appears that natural beings can stand limited and harmonized in relation to one another and the whole.

It is not impossible to confuse such an orientalizing limitation of technological naturalism with a division in medieval Catholic theology of the Trinitarian principle from the finite or natural and the knowlege thereof. There is, however, the immense difference that the principle is there understood to be concrete and creative of nature. The principle is not Being only but Being that is self-conscious and providentially creative. And the categories of the finite are not altogether a barrier to speaking of the principle, since they are understood as a way of being of the infinite reason. Into this medieval theology has gone the philosophic work of the Greeks which had for its result to equalize being and thinking.

The modern comes, however, to this theology, and to the Christian tradition more generally, with the secular forms dependent on it – the family, political freedom, etc – by way of technological naturalism. The negation of that, one may say, is often for him the convincing mediation and proof of the tradition, toward which he may assume a more or less conservative attitude. The difficulty in this is that his relation to the content of the tradition is highly abstract and formal. He has the content in a certain aesthetic relation, through image, ceremony, and the like, and not rationally, as was sought in the tradition in the times of its vitality. No more than the content of the Christian religion can European secularity be known in its true nature in this external and naturalistic attitude. That may continue to be done which has been done traditionally. The customary may be kept in existence down to its most local and particular ramifications. But the customary as merely existent is not law in either a Hebrew or a Roman sense and is not ethical in the Greek sense – the concretion of the universal and the natural. The mere continuance of the old and customary has no power to educate, but can only impart an external order to the savagery of the natural will. The total confusion of good and evil in the technological naturalism – where what impedes the natural is called evil and the natural called good in its opposition to reason – is here abated. For not the natural but Being is first, and in the natural is sought not only itself but also some presence of Being – a formal beauty.

In the separating of Being from the finite and the incipient limiting of the natural appears the true character of the Nietzschean or anti-technological naturalism. It is not a saving of the natural but the beginning of a conversion from it to the universal and intelligible. To the European or North American it can appear that he has fled the destructive rationalism of technology and from Nietzsche has learned the true natural individuality. The cultures and religions of the Far East, which have a like logical structure, attract him similarly as more natural than his own. So it appears while he is in revolt against the Christian tradition and in that opposition has gone over to nature. His flight, however, from the impossibility of a natural or immediate accommodation of nature and reason – from technological naturalism – is properly a giving up of that revolt, in that not natural individuality but an objective and universal principle is taken to be first. There remains, however, a certain ambiguity so long as one orientalizes in the interest of a Christian and European tradition and not for itself. The European or North American is in the curious relation to his religion and culture that he would have them while at the same time being in revolt against them. There is need of the experience that the abstract principle that should sustain this relation has rather the consequence of destroying it.

One may study Indian and other Far Eastern thought from the standpoint of the technological reason that can set itself beyond every content and in all discover in truth only its own formal identity. Or one can look to find some limit there and be still in that relation a good European. Another matter is to take this thought on its own account – to measure the natural and particular by the principle or principles that there appear. By this measure the free, natural individuality of the European decadence has no truth. Its origin was indeed in Christian belief and thought, so that it should not seem wonderful if it is not confirmed in other and more abstract principles. All that tradition and its classical and Hebrew antecedents become problematical in this context, and the dead habitual assumption that somehow they belong to the naturalistic individual can be questioned. There begins the possibility of philosophy again, a forgotten art since Marx, as he thought, set Hegel on his feet – or another elsewhere did the like – and philosophy became an ever indeterminate, open debate.

It is not that Christians and Europeans are likely to abandon their concrete principle. The knowledge of it was lost to them, however, so far as nation, culture, language, and other natural particularities, and concentration of them all in natural individuality became the medium through which the universal was known. It is a right instinct of reason that in the very effort to hold to these particularities it regains a relation to the universal as principle.

It is with difficulty that those who adhere to something of a Christian and European tradition admit so radical a criticism of natural subjectivity. Instead one prefers some part of the tradition to another as more natural and less nearly surrendered to technology. One returns to Orthodoxy, another to the early Middle Ages, in general to where the Christian principle had not yet made itself deeply felt against a barbarous will. Or in the practical realm one would somewhere arrest the attainment of free government, whether the American revolution was already an excess of freedom, or first the French, or only some later disturbance. But in such preferences it is overlooked that the measure applied is the decadent natural subjectivity, which is more at home in fancy in some historical mansions than in others. Perhaps only some parts of the tradition have succumbed to the naturalistic principle, but all show themselves vulnerable to it.

One need not think the decay of the tradition in its older forms wholly a loss. We are perhaps related to our particular national and religious histories somewhat as the free states of classical antiquity, whose political decline was the beginning of a reflection on their past and the formation of the universal culture that became the education of Christian times. We are far from such a knowledge of the Christian belief and its secularity, but perhaps begin to be capable of it. The subjective, individualistic revolt in which we still live – the modern sophistry it might be called – is not against the tradition as such, of which it has no grasp, but rather against particular historical forms. There is in it a perception of their limit, as in the conflict of Christian sects, each calling itself alone Catholic or in the warring of Christian states. The subjective revolt or decadence may be thought implicitly a purgation from such absolute particularities.

A consequence of the lapse into natural subjectivity is that primitive peoples are drawn into our cultural world, and not in a reflective relation to the noble savage, as in the eighteenth century, but by a total submission to the primitive. The black African is much more a cultural model than the classical Greek or a medieval European. Likewise the great cultures of the Far East, beyond the ancient peoples of the Mediterranean area from whom Christian Europe drew its religion and culture, are no longer external, but may be said to have taken their rude conquerors captive. For it is with them especially that one finds the state of being in nature while related to an abstract principle that is congenial to Europeans and North Americans as they raise their heads from technological naturalism.

What peoples of European and Christian tradition are peculiarly ignorant of and oblivious to is first the rational cultures of classical antiquity and then the deeper intellectuality of the Christian tradition itself. One comes to this study presupposing a natural subjectivity and understands just as much as follows from this presupposition. What is of interest, however, and chiefly important to learn, is how this beginning was there experienced as untrue and the natural led back to the universal as its principle. The forgetting of our tradition is not altogether as Heidegger describes it. His thought is contracted excessively into an opposition to technological naturalism, where already one had turned from classical and Christian rationality.

On that account, returning rightly to Parmenides and Heraclitus, he finds every advance from it rather a descent back to abstract reason. But the overcoming of technological naturalism is not in that immediacy but in a concrete intellectuality, as in classical and Christian thought. To regain a knowledge of this thought – and better founded than the older knowledge of it – appears to be the principal intellectual work of the present time. It was said that the Christian religion came 'in the fullness of time,' that is, as mediated by antecedent religions and cultures. Out of the fall back to immediacy the need, if one would know this religion and its secular implications truly, is to come to a more accurate knowledge of this mediation.

IV

So far as Canadians assume the free natural individuality of socialism and modern liberation to be the true principle of political association,

they will reasonably be guided by its implications when they consider
the form of their government internally and their relation to the
United States. These implications appear to be estimated quite well by
pragmatic politicians. One will not mistake English-Canadian or French-
Canadian nationalism for more than it is: a fascistic, fanatical force, if
encouraged by deep resentments; weaker otherwise than private economic interest. One will recognize as inevitable on this principle a pol-
arization of society into abstract, technocratic bureaucracy and anarchic,
natural individuality. To satisfy the second there is need of decentral-
ization, of giving room to linguistic, cultural, regional differences. In
this way the hostility of anarchic individuals to bureaucracy can be
somewhat placated. But the more that is conceded to natural particularities, the more complex, costly, oppressive government must become.
To suppose one of these directions possible without the other betrays
ignorance of the principle assumed.

The perils of such government are not unknown. The demand is
made that government be open – freedom of information – but, in pro-
portion as it is open, it will be more secret, as ever when there is an
approximation to direct democracy. Open government in a true sense
supposes an ordered relation between individuals and state. Without
this relation representative bodies – parliaments – are capable only of
endless debate and can become as irrelevant as the Roman Senate
under the Empire. Such a police state as the Soviet Union is possible
because between government and people there is not an ordered,
rational mediation of differences, but abstract, statistical, computer
reason, which easily has need of terror and compulsion. And in general
there is a perverse ignorance of human evil, as spoken of already, such
as in some circumstances can bring a Hitler or Stalin to power, and
appears in many other ways.

The United States will not reasonably seem foreign to free, natural
individuals but rather their spiritual fatherland. Now that it has gone
natural, one may expect the same decentralizing tendency as in Canada – and a respect for linguistic and other natural differences as in
Canada. This tendency will be contradicted, as in Canada, by technocratic bureaucracy, which will certainly be oppressive.

Language and culture on this principle are natural rights. As such
they fall to the anarchic pole of the technological society. They are

therefore insufficient grounds for independence from the bureaucratic state. So far as they are liberated, natural individuals, the Québécois will consistently acquiesce in the Canadian confederation, if it does not impede the non-political enjoyment of these rights.

Whether Canadians have, on the whole, gone over to this technological naturalism and how long, if they have, they are likely to remain of this mind, there is no way of estimating. It is acquiesced in, no doubt, and might be discovered to be our culture by opinion polls. But as our colonial attachments to an older culture were borrowed, so also is our attachment to its decadence. Since the Hitler war all the latest fashions of European and American thought have been brought to Canada, largely by academics of foreign birth. Our artists give to international trends a Canadian setting. Canadians have become sophisticated, and in that is some gain as against the older colonial mentality. But this is the affair of a prosperous middle class, toward which most are indifferent.

This naturalistic individualism Americans take up with a passion. It is an easy extension and seeming fulfilment of their former revolution. To it, in its various pious and impious forms, they bring a moral passion and are wonderfully able to think themselves the end of creation, as the principle assumes, and to evade the evil in it. This revolutionary passion is un-Canadian. A sceptical, indifferent acceptance of the gifts foreigners bring is more typically Canadian.

Canadians do not have the resource of an established national culture that permits Europeans to a degree to live in the old and the new, to preserve something of old habits and cultivation while they indulge in the barbarism of technological individualism. This division is less easy and near impossible for Canadians because they are not a nation in the European sense. Our culture is not a historical growth, but a relation to the historical culture, already complete, of Britain, France, or other European nations. What is called Canadian history is partly our relation to external nature, partly the process of our reception of European culture to the point of political independence. The possession and retention of a cultivated life have another character for Canadians than for Europeans in their decadence. They are different also from those of Americans, for whom the basis of whatever else they receive appears to be the strong individualism of their revolutionary culture. Canadians are unformed and do not thus put their imprint on what they receive.

It is generally thought that Canadians, whether English-speaking or French-speaking, have not much will to Americanize. If this means, as it may, that, however inarticulately, they are too strongly drawn to an older Christian and European culture to revel in the free, natural individuality of contemporary Americans, then it is possible to define the peculiar quality of being Canadian. The problem is set for them that either they can be nothing, ever receptive and imitative, or they can define their rejection of technological naturalism by means of the old tradition. To that tradition and the rational freedom it contains their relation is commonly nostalgic: it is not their actual culture. It is not impossible that it should be their actual culture, and there is quite certainly no other way of repelling the servitude of free, natural individuality or technology. But whether the desire of rational freedom will ever be strong is so apathetic a people, none can say.

To the problems of the Canadian federation a less melancholy solution than that before described might sometime be possible if the principle of political association were not natural individuality, but a common attachment to rational institutions, as in the older tradition. On that basis linguistic and cultural differences could subsist not as natural rights only but could have a political and educative power as well.

JOHN G. ARAPURA

Modern thought and the transcendent: Some observations based on an Eastern view

In modern philosophy notions of the transcendent are under attack. Some philosophers have put them aside, others have positively ignored them, and yet others have openly rejected them. Of course, there are also some great thinkers such as Martin Heidegger who have given us new interpretations of the transcendent from their own very profound standpoints. However, even at the beginning we cannot avoid ironies. Is it possible, in a strange way, that the one who originally denied the transcendent to reason (Kant) still preserved the Eternal, while another who held the transcendent up to thought (Heidegger) let go of the Eternal?

In modern thought in general, not just in philosophy but in the wider field led or even followed by philosophy, the transcendent has been allowed to suffer attrition. The most dominant trend in all modern thought, namely, positivism, involves a radical turning away from the Eternal and the transcendent. In the face of it new expressions of profundities involving the question of being and hence the transcendent would appear to be a mere change of pace in a world too impatient to be held up unduly by matters that are not taken seriously any more. But then those who have the patience and requisite turn of mind to join in thinking about such matters do not feel justified in ignoring them.

Modern thought undoubtedly is Western not only in its origin but in its direction as well. Nevertheless no part of the world is any longer outside its embrace. Even the most sophisticated of Eastern cultures are waking up to the fact that something powerful has hit them. They notice, of course, the most obvious expressions of it, in Marxist revolution and technology particularly, which are both Western in origin, but often they do not see much of what lies behind these conspicuous expressions.

But some indeed do see it. And many of those who see do not react at all while those who react do so diversely. There are out and out Eastern protagonists of modernity who never ask any deep questions but speak and act as though acceptance of modernity is a matter of simple technical and external adjustment. Then there are two types of more serious people, who are rather given to apologetic interpretation and applied thought than to anything else. Here interpretation may take place in either direction. In other words, some people put modern Western thought in some traditional Eastern package, while others try to package traditional Eastern thought in the language and the categories of the modern West. As for the latter group, again, what is selected by each person as typically Eastern or Western will depend upon his own interest and bias. By and large, it is said that Chinese scholars are given to presenting Western thought in Chinese dress (to their own people, of course), while Indian scholars are apt to engage in expressing Indian thought in Western language and idiom. Both of these types of activity require the selection of parallels from the East and the West. And parallels, however superficial, are available in large quantities.

Let us turn to another kind of possible Eastern reaction, a genuine philosophical response. Now, this is very difficult. In talking about a philosophical response, are we not supposed to have an agreed upon understanding as to what philosophy is? And certainly one should not try to take advantage of the fact that there is no definition of philosophy on which all have agreed. Historically, philosophy is a Western phenomenon. There are even questions as to whether there is philosophy outside the West. Even such a great figure as Heidegger writes that philosophy is only Western 'and there is no other, neither a Chinese nor an Indian Philosophy' (*What Is Called Thinking*? trans J.G. Gray [New York: Harper 1968] 224; *Was Heisst Denken*? [Tübingen 1961] 134–5). However, even if this contention were true in a narrow sense, by excluding certain highly specialized and sustained Eastern intellectual enterprises we miss a supreme chance to arrive at some profound understanding and possibly a definition of what philosophy is.

When we try to define philosophy we find that we have to look at something elusive at the very centre of the philosophical enterprise: Is coming to know or at least to deal with the transcendent essential to philosophy? The fundamental controversy in modern philosophy is really about this question, although it may appear in several different garbs. No definition of philosophy is possible without including a resolution of this problem, and none exists. Accordingly, the very definition of philosophy must take into account the issue of the expulsion of the transcendent from modern thought. Any consideration of this issue implicitly does so, and even when we are trying only to define philosophy our effort is likewise implicitly tied to the issue of the transcendent. Surely there are other such controversial issues linked with the project of defining philosophy, but this is the most central.

In grappling with the transcendent or in defining philosophy, the Vedanta can be of great help. Its absolute certainty about Ultimate Reality (*Brahman*) has the power to ignite in new ways the philosophical problem of the transcendent.

Now, in view of Kant's special use of the term 'transcendent' and the consequent association of that special meaning to the word in later philosophy, it is necessary to make some preliminary remarks. The transcendent is to Kant a false dimension that reason in its pre-critical arrogance assumes, whereby it fancies that it knows what is beyond its power to know, namely the Ultimately Real or things-in-themselves. Hence he condemns it as a false principle (cf *Critique of Pure Reason* second edition, A296, B353, trans N.K. Smith, 299). Because he is dealing with the transcendent in the context of epistemology, he is talking about knowledge in the sense of knowing the real that is out there. He left the real in its complete aura of sacredness, without allowing it to be touched with anything from here. The transcendent, accordingly, is understood as the principle of pre-critical reason's moving from here to a beyond that is out there. The distance between here and there, he felt, is immeasurable. Into that gap faith is introduced as a matter of practical reason. 'I have therefore found it necessary to deny knowledge in order to make room for faith,' he writes (preface to *Critique of Pure Reason* 2).

The Vedanta takes a very different approach. It is not talking about a beyond measured from here to an unbounded 'there.' It is reversing the base of the projection, from a definite there to an indeterminate (anirvacanīya) here. It is as impressed as Kant was about the sheer unknowability of the Real. It puts forward the remarkable thesis that the Ultimately Real is unknowable for the utterly paradoxical reason that it is knowledge (gnosis) itself. Śankara defines the Vedanta as philosophy in a breath-takingly simple and direct fashion: 'It is the vision of the principle of Ultimate Reality wherein is no distinction of knowledge, known and knower' (jñāna-jneya-jñātr-bhedarahitamparamartha-tattva-darśanam) (Commentary on the Māndūkya Kārikā 4.1). Jnana, translated 'gnosis,' and philologically cognate with it, primarily describes the disposition of the Ultimately Real within itself, and secondarily means our knowledge of the Ultimately Real by virtue of that same disposition. Darśana, literally 'vision,' 'view,' 'perception,' has the primary meaning 'theoria' and the secondary meaning 'theory' (which is itself metamorphosed from 'theoria'). In the latter sense it is being used as a word by which to translate 'philosophy.' The compound word tattva-darśana, that is, darśana of tattva or principle can also be used in a primary or a secondary sense. However, jñāna and darśana are identical only for the secondary meaning of the former and the primary meaning of the latter. Also, in popular parlance words, even the highest, are seldom preserved in their pristine usages but often stretched out into secondary or tertiary employment. Such an extension is evident in the case of jñāna. It is used for any knowledge, particularly for cognition. It is also used in lieu of darśana or philosophy. But in the compound form tattva-jñāna it has been invariably used in the same sense, exactly like tattva-darśana.

But let us return to the essential meaning of jñāna as gnosis, the Ultimately Real's disposition in itself. Clearly, the word 'disposition' is a metaphor, and there is no way of getting beyond metaphors when we are speaking about the Ultimately Real. When we say 'There is no way of getting beyond metaphors,' we must not take this as the doom of thought or its eternal confinement to a terrestrial orbit. On the contrary, metaphor can bring our release toward that about which we speak, namely the Ultimately Real. But we must not confuse the use of metaphors with comprehension or description of the real thing.

When we speak metaphorically of the disposition of the Ultimately Real in itself, we understand this disposition to be as it is toward us. This kind of disposition or dispositional activity is what is expressed by the Upanisadic-Vedantic usage of the word *iccha* and its variants, such as *iksana* and *iksitrtva*. It stands for the very ground of the activities that we know diversely as thinking, willing, desiring. It is also the activity by which things come to be. We find references to it in the Upanisads, most notably in *Chandogya* 6.2.3, *Aitareya* 1.1.1, and *Prasna* 6.3. In that way gnosis is an activity, not in the ordinary sense of moving toward a goal or executing a purpose, but rather in a metaphorical sense. But the metaphor must not be taken to mean a mere figure of speech. Texts of the Vedanta take special care to say that the activity of gnosis is not such a figure of speech, called *gauna* in Indian theories of meaning. Referring to such activity, the statement in *Vedanta Sutra* 1.1.6 – *gaunascet na atmasabdat* (Is it a mere figure of speech? No, because of the word Atman.) – settles it. Sankara, commenting on it, demonstrates the profound connection of such activity with Being (*sat*) itself and writes: 'Because the word Atman is employed in reference to it *iksitrtva* is not used as a figure of speech (here).' Therefore, it is a metaphor in the deepest sense of the word.

Heidegger's comment on Kant is illuminating: 'If what Kant terms "our thought" is this pure self-orienting reference ... the "thinking" of such a thought is not an act of judgement but is thinking in the sense of the free, but not arbitrary "envisioning" (Sich-denken) of something, an envisioning which is at once a forming and a projecting. This primordial act of "thinking" is an act of pure imagination' (*Kant and the Problem of Metaphysics* trans J.S. Churchill [Bloomington: Indiana University Press 1962] 158; cf German original, 139). But who is the thinker in this thinking? Or is it a mere subjectless activity? There is a thin line between metaphor and figure of speech, and yet it is also the widest gulf and therefore the most perilous. The Vedanta always insists that it is important to look at the other side of a metaphor to see what it is a metaphor of, as otherwise it could easily become a mere figure of speech emphasizing nothing but thought's 'self-orienting reference.' Heidegger has shown us the great depth of what is called thought and

has shown in a masterly way that thinking is not grasping or appre-
hending but rather a receptivity to what lies before us (for instance see
Kant and the Problem of Metaphysics 160; *What Is Called Thinking?*
trans J.G. Gray [New York: Harper 1968] 211). In the light of the
Vedanta, one has to ask whether what lies before us has the character
of gnosis, in which the very conjunction of *legein* and *noein* as the
fundamental character of thinking that Heidegger speaks about (*What
Is Called Thinking?* 211) is made possible. Does not receptivity itself,
by definition not an activity, presuppose an activity elsewhere, which is
none other than gnosis?

As far as the Vedanta is concerned, the metaphor of gnosis being its
own activity is important also for negating the impression that the
knowledge of the Eternal that man gains is the result of any activity on
his part. Śankara writes 'The science of the knowledge of Brahman
does not depend upon any activity on the part of man, (in other words
it is not *puruṣa-vyāpāra-tantra*),' (*Commentary on the Vedānta Sūtras*
1.1.4). Gnosis is never produced; it is what is there, inseparable from
the Eternal or Ultimately Real.

The Vedanta, beginning from the Upaniṣads, uses the analogy of
light to describe gnosis. Brahman is the light of lights, *jyotiṣām jyotiḥ*
(*Bṛhadāraṇyaka Upaniṣad* 4.4.16, 3.9.10). Everything is at sometime or
other spoken of as light. Gnosis is described as the transcendent self-
shining light of Brahman. There never was any need to establish the
existence of the transcendent self-shining light. On the contrary, its
self-evidence was demonstrated on the ground that all other evidences
depend on it. This is the unique procedure of reasoning that the
Vedanta in its scholastic development carried out to perfection. Onto-
logically there never was any attempt to prove the transcendent. On
the contrary, the way chosen was to let it demonstrate itself as the sole
ground (*ādhāra*) of all things. However, we will not enter the vast and
intricate debate between the Vedanta and opposing schools such as the
Nyaya on what came to be advanced as the doctrine of self-luminosity
(*svaprakāśa*), as these opposing schools rejected it and proposed their
own doctrine of other-luminosity (*paratah-prakāśa*).

Surely modern thought is a far cry from self-luminosity. Thus, when
the Vedanta joins in a philosophical response to modern thought, par-

ticularly in the context of the modern expulsion of the transcendent from the ground of knowledge, it is bound to base its stand on its unique views of gnosis and self-light. It is bound to be at odds with the basis of contemporary epistemology, with its views of positivist rationality. The latter assumes that our primary task in the pursuit of knowledge is executed by what is most tellingly called research, that is to say, our own bringing a little light into an inherently dark situation. There is no longer any notion of a general light that shines apart from our efforts, in which things can be *dis-covered*.

The turn away from the transcendent accords with the rejection of the notions of any general light that exists out there. Yet there is a parallel between Western and Vedantic thought in the Appearance-Reality metaphysics grounded in Kant's *Critiques*. A century of comparative scholarship on the Vedanta has assumed, based on a striking similarity of language and even of method between some works of the Vedanta and Kant, that the Vedanta espouses an Appearance-Reality metaphysics. But there is a significant difference.

In the Vedanta only Brahman the Ultimately Real shines by itself; nothing else shines by itself, but all things shine *in* the light of Brahman. As the *Muṇḍaka Upaniṣad* 2.2.10 and 11 has it: 'In the transcendent golden sheath is Brahman without taint, without parts. Pure it is, light of lights. That is what the knowers of the Ātman know. There the sun shines not, nor the moon, nor the stars, these lightnings shine not. So whence could this fire be? Everything shines only after that shining light. His shining lightens this whole universe.' Commenting on the phrase 'Everything shines only after that shining light,' Śankara writes, 'In the light of that (Ātman) alone everything that is not – Atman shines as it does not have power to shine by itself (*tasyai'va bhāsā sarvam anyad anātma-jātam prakāśyati, na tu tasya svataḥ prakāśana sāmarthyam)*.'

In contrast, the Kantian doctrine seems to say that things that appear to us are dark, and we can see only darkly, because of our limited capacity for experience and the limited power of our reason, and as for the things-in-themselves there is no hint of any light of their own reaching us. In some sense this doctrine seems to be the very obverse of the Vedanta.

It was Paul Deussen, the great German scholar of the Vedanta and a close friend of Nietzsche, who wrote and worked on the assumption of a similarity between Parmenides, Kant, and Śankara. Deussen argued that Kant's teaching that 'the world reveals to us appearances only and not the being of things-in-themselves' is exactly the same as Śankara's (see *The System of the Vedanta* trans Charles Johnston [Delhi: Moltilal Banarsidass 19] 48]. Deussen set a pattern that is still very much in vogue.

Nietzsche, after reading Deussen's *Das System des Vedanta*, wrote to him[1] that having read the book page for page he found that his position was 'Yes where your book says No.' Nietzsche read some works of the Vedanta at first hand also, and he rejected that system for the same reason he rejected Kant. He writes: 'At bottom Kant wanted to prove that starting from the subject the subject could not be proved – nor could the object; the possibility of a merely apparent existence (Scheinexistenz) of the subject, "the soul" in other words, may not always have remained strange to him – that thought as Vedanta philosophy existed once before on this earth and exercised tremendous power' (*Beyond Good and Evil* trans Walter Kaufmann, [New York: Vintage Books, 1966] 67).

The mistake of treating the Vedanta in terms of Appearance-Reality will become clear as we probe the idea of the self-shining of Brahman. The locus classicus of the idea is in *Bṛhadāraṇyaka* 4.3.1–6. Here different sources of light by which we can see things and are able to move about are discussed: the sun, the moon, fire, and speech itself. The question finally is raised as to what happens in a condition in which all these various sources of light are no longer available. 'When the sun has set, Yājnavalkya, and the moon has set and fire has gone out and speech has become silent, what light does a person here have? "Ātman indeed is the light," said he, "for Ātman as light one sits, moves around, goes about one's work and returns."'

Among the most typical words for light are *jyotiḥ* and *bhāḥ*. In one place these two are used together, *svena bhāsā, svena jyotiṣā* (by his own shining, by his own light) (*Bṛhadāraṇyaka* 4.3.9). The stem *bhā* is cognate with the Greek *pha*. *Bhā* is of particular importance because of what we can learn from its Greek parallel and also because it is picked out for analysis in the *Maitrī Upaniṣad* 4.7. (*Bhā* means 'he that illumines these worlds.')

Heidegger discusses words from the Greek stem *pha*. We are struck by the great similarity. To quote a lengthy passage from Heidegger: 'The Greek expression φαινόμενον, to which the term "phenomenon" goes back, is derived from the word φαίνεσθαι, which signifies "to show itself". Thus φαινόμενον means that which shows itself, the manifest [das, was sich zeigt, das Sichzeigende, das Offenbare] φαίνεσθαι itself is a middle-voiced form which comes from φαίνω to bring to the light of day, to put in the light. φαίνω comes from the stem φα like φως, the light, that which is bright, in other words, that wherein something can become manifest, visible in itself. Thus we must *keep in mind* that the expression "phenomenon" signifies that which shows itself in itself, the manifest.' *Being and Time* trans J. Macquarrie and E. Robinson (New York: Harper 1962) 51

In view of this the doctrine of Appearance (*Erscheinung*) as against Reality may have something to do with extending the concept of phenomenon in a new direction. Heidegger points out that 'phenomenon' has two significations, the first being 'that which shows itself' and the second 'that which shows itself as something which it is not, and therefore merely looking like so-and-so or semblance.' The first is the primordial signification, and the second is founded on it. But Heidegger states that neither has anything to do with what is called 'an appearance' and still less 'a mere appearance.'

In the Vedanta too all this is true. Light (*bhāḥ*, *jyotiḥ*, etc) has the primary and secondary significations that Heidegger's discussion of 'phenomenon' points out. There is also a seeming appearance, which is illustrated by the rope-snake analogy. But there is no such thing as a mere appearance without a transcendent substratum. A mere appearance is a mere illusion and has no status whatsoever. *Māyā*, which is indefinable (*anirvcanīya*), is itself a phenomenon in the proper sense, a manifestation of the Ultimately Real. Even in the condition of *māyā* (which is the totality of all conditions) there is the possibility of transcendental certainty as to the Eternal. The work of philosophy is to show the way to that certainty. It inculcates only that certainty through exegesis of Being which is aimed at the removal of the veiling ignorance (avidyā) that obscures the unity of one's own being with Brahman. Śankara writes about the discipline of this philosophy (technically śāstra): 'It propounds Brahman as not being an object but as being the universal Self and thereby removes the distinction between the known, the knower and knowledge' (Commentary on Vedānta Sūtras 1.1.4). Clearly, transcendental certainty is not outside the condition called māyā but within it. Outside māyā there is no need for philosophy or even for certainty. It will be gnosis itself.

Now, is this transcendental certainty dogmatism? Nietzsche would describe it as such: 'It seems that all great things first have to bestride the earth in monstrous and frightening masks (Fratzen) in order to inscribe themselves in the hearts of humanity with eternal demands: dogmatic philosophy was such a mask; for example the Vedanta doctrine in Asia and Platonism in Europe' (preface to Beyond Good and Evil 67).

Now that we have come to Nietzsche and his reaction to the Vedanta, it is time to throw away all the books and speak a few words in aphorisms, and then conclude. I am not able to speak for Platonism and so will confine myself to the Vedanta. But it would seem that what is applicable to the one is in large measure applicable to the other as well.

If the Vedanta seems to be dogmatic it is for reasons diametrically opposed to those on which dogmatism is usually founded. Even if the Vedanta be dogmatic it is so only for matters of a transcendent nature. If one has to be dogmatic at all it is perhaps better to be dogmatic on such matters than on worldly things based on empirical assumptions or dialectical laws of history.

The transcendent without the immanent is benign. But the immanent without the transcendent is only harmless at best; without the transcendent the immanent has no bite.

When an immanentist doctrine assumes the character of transcendental certainty it has to trade knowledge for power. Then it becomes a tiger with whom it is hard to live and dangerous to lie down.

The transcendent is the only defence against the tyrannies of history and against history itself, which is probably the greatest of all tyrannies because it is the most transcendental form that immanentist reason arrogates to itself.

The transcendent is the only true friend of the friendless. It alone keeps our secrets. Because of it what can never be spoken is also spoken.

Atheism, whatever it is, is a friend of the immanent gods. The transcendent is never a god.

There are three forms of temporal immanentism: past (history), present (social reality), and future (technology). Those who are consumed by any of these are usually hostile to the Eternal, while those who are consumed by the Eternal are always benevolently disposed to these three realms.

Total concentration on the immanent makes the immanent monstrous and diabolical. It generates the tyranny of immediacy, which is impatience with the need to be patient, with delay of fulfilment, in fact frustration of transcendence itself. Do not call it freedom.

If we have to choose between transcendental certainty and immanental uncertainty on the one hand and transcendental uncertainty and immanent certainty on the other, it is far better to choose the former.

Immanental uncertainty, that is, uncertainty about what is before us, is one of the highest gifts of the Eternal, if it already cohabits with transcendental certainty. There is no room for dogmatism here.

Transcendental certainty is to the Knowledge of the Good what the Categorical Imperative is to the knowledge of what ought to be done. Both are above dogmatism. Besides, because of transcendental certainty the Categorical Imperative will be able to bring forth noble deeds. This age especially cries for noble deeds.

NOTE

1 For information regarding exchanges between Nietzsche and Deussen, I am indebted to a seminar paper written by Hans Rollman of McMaster University, 'Deussen, Nietzsche and Vedanta.'

JAN YÜN-HUA

Confucian tradition and modernity: A dilemma on both sides

The purpose of this essay is to discuss the conflict between the traditional and technology and its consequences as experienced in the Chinese context. From the early decades of the present century, many Chinese scholars have expressed their concerns and debated among themselves on this problem. A review of their debates will be useful to our reflections on this vital but difficult question.

At the time when China was forced by gunboats and technology into the modern age, the Confucian way of life was the dominant force in the country. All those who have advocated a modernization of China have blamed the Confucian tradition as the cause of China's backwardness. In their view, China could be strong only if she accepted 'Western' civilization totally, without any reservation. The concept of modernity to them meant the seeking of material well-being, the overcoming of ignorance through modern education, the discovery of truth, the invention of techniques and machinery, the conquest of nature, a change of systems, and the spirit of revolution.[1] In the words of a radical revolutionary, modernity means a cultural and scientific new democracy, which opposes 'all feudal and superstitious thought; it advocates practical realism, objective truth, and the union of theory and practice.'[2] From this point of view, the Chinese concept of modernity involved a total change of thought, of modes of production, and of the socio-political system as well as of the whole way of life and outlook on the world. The principal difference between the traditional Confucian and the new intelligentsia was that the former was oriented toward the past, and the latter toward the future. This conflicting orientation, along with the immense and urgent pressure of foreign invasion, especially from the imperialist Japanese military, forced China to look for a short-term, radical change, so that she could survive the invasion.

The image of the Confucian tradition being oriented toward the past was created both by the Confucian concept of Chinese history and by its connection with the Chinese bureaucracy of the past and of the early years of the republic. Government patronage of Confucianism in imperial and republican China made the tradition an inevitable target.

MODERNIST CRITICISM

The principal difference between the modern and traditional critics of Confucianism is their focus of attention. To the old anti-Confucian philosophers, the focal point is culture; to the modernists, it is economics, especially economic production. The modernists' anti-Confucian critique began with the writings of Ch'en Tu-hsiu (1879–1942), the founder of the Chinese Communist party who was later purged as a Trotskyist. His essay 'The Way of Confucius and Modern Life'[3] initiated the attack on Confucian tradition from both the social and the ethical viewpoint.

Socially, he attacked the Confucian teaching of proprieties (li-chiao) as superfluous, cruel, and harmful to the Chinese outlook and hence unsuitable for a modern society. It was superfluous because it insisted on the old tradition but disregarded completely the needs of the present society. It was cruel because the proprieties were usually one-sided in favour of a privileged few – rulers, fathers, husbands, and elders – at the expense of subject, son and daughter, wife and youth. Under the name of proprieties, social institutions killed thousands of oppressed people. It was unsuitable for a modern society, which demanded individual freedom, struggle and competition in material culture, and new social mores; the feudal relationship between privileged and under-privileged in the Confucian tradition did not allow the majority of society freedom to act. The immediacy of this institutional aspect of tradition in Chinese life he saw as the basis of despotism.

Confucian ethics of filial piety (hsiao) and blind loyalty (chung) were at the core of traditional Chinese society. The critic pointed out sharply that the norm of the Book of Rites, which says, 'While parents are living, the son dares not regard his person or property as his own,' or that 'the son should not deviate from the father's way even three years after his death,'[4] is absolutely contradictory to all modern constitutions. Similarly, the doctrine that 'the rules of decorum do not go down to the common people and the penal statutes do not go up to great officers' does not have a place in a modern society. Another modernist critic, Wu Yü, had the same view on Confucian ethics and criticized them more fiercely. He inveighed against not only the obstructive ideas of the Confucian teaching of proprieties, but also against the social institutions that carried out its ethical principles. He agreed that filial piety is not only applied to Chinese families, but is also the basis of the principle of unquestioning loyalty.[5] These 'virtues' made Chinese youth obedient sons in the house, daring not to offend their superiors or to be rebellious. The effect of this idea was to make China a great factory which produced nothing but obedient subjects.

Politically, a modern society is based on individual freedom and rights, while the Confucian tradition insists on feudal relationships based upon units of family and clan, which negate individual freedom and rights. The critics also objected to the Confucian caste system in which there was great inequality in individual status, i.e. ruler-subject, father-son, husband-wife. Such a system was feudalistic in nature and had no place in modern political institutions.[6]

Criticism continued in the following decades and intensified before the Communists took over China. Through the process of this continuous confrontation, the contents of the anti-Confucian criticism became more elaborated and focused. Tsai Shang-ssu's book *A General Critique to Traditional Chinese Thought*[7] may be regarded as a conclusive criticism of Confucian tradition before the rise of Communism in China. Ts'ai Shang-ssu's study is an all-out attack on tradition. The author claims that tradition is the enemy of labour and peasants and a friend of the rich and privileged. It is an enemy of women, society, democracy, civilization, the scientific spirit, truth, and the creative revolution. In contrast, Confucianism is a friend of male chauvinists, the family or clan, the dictator, and the uncivilized, and artificial, and it clings to the past.

In another chapter, the author points out the incompatibilities between Confucianism and the 'new age.' He describes Confucian tradition as anti-democratic in politics, anti-egalitarian in economics, anti-social in morality, anti-natural in sciences, anti-materialistic in history, and anti-scientific in research. Although the headings look propagandistic, the book presents the modernist viewpoint clearly and with some substance. Compared to earlier modernists' attacks on Confucian tradition, the book is highly systematic in its arguments.

The author describes Confucianism as anti-democratic in order to attack the then-current Confucian interpretation of the tradition as itself democratic, based on Confucius's statement 'Do not concern yourself with matters of government unless they are the responsibility of your office.'[8] The author criticizes the teaching as passive and an inhibition to politics. Moreover, Confucius also said that a gentleman has three fears: 'He is in awe of the Decree of Heaven. He is in awe of great men. He is in awe of the words of the sages.'[9] In contrast, 'the small man, being ignorant of the Decree of Heaven, does not stand in awe of it. He treats great men with insolence and the words of the sages with derision.'[10] These and similar passages in the Confucian classics were used as evidence that Confucius advocated dictatorial politics.

The criticism of Confucian tradition as 'anti-egalitarian in economics' is a refutation of a modern interpretation. According to some modern Confucian scholars, Confucianism is similar or even better than socialism. This interpretation has become a block to the advocates of modernity. The interpretation is based on a statement from *Analects*: 'The head of a state or a noble family worries not about underpopulation but about uneven distribution, not about poverty but about instability. For where there is even distribution there is no such thing as poverty, where there is stability there is no such thing as overturning.'[11] The Confucianists usually give a liberal reading to this passage, while the modernists insist that it is descriptive and merely points out that excessive riches make men arrogant, while poverty makes men worry. The advice given by the passage is a soft reformation, aimed at harmony and equal distribution, so that the ruler may easily govern the masses. However, the modernist sees no concrete program set out as to how to distribute the wealth equally. Moreover, the radicals were convinced that only a revolution could solve China's problems. Reformations, especially such as advocated by Confucianists, are not merely incapable of rescuing the country, but would delude the people from their concentration on revolution and economic advancement.

The criticism of Confucian tradition as anti-scientific is mainly a critique of the Confucian emphasis on human relationships. The modernists have pointed out that Confucian classics such as *Analects*, *Mencius*, and *Book of Change* concentrate on human relations and pay not the slightest attention to nature. One classical Confucian interpreter, Tung Chung-shu (ca 179–ca 104 BC), stated: 'Topics such as the discussion on birds and animals are not what the sage wished to discuss. What the sage wanted to discuss is the principle of humanity (jen) and righteousness (yi). If this is not the case, then one would show interest in various words and things, and thus talk on a subject that is not urgent. Is this not a serious matter which confuses young scholars and is hated by gentlemen?'[12] The modernists conclude that the main cause of China's backwardness in natural science is the Confucian over-emphasis on human relations and its negligence of nature.

The all-out attack on Confucian tradition reached its peak in the early 1970s, during the Cultural Revolution. Although the campaign was largely an internal power struggle among Communist leaders, it started with a criticism of Confucianism. The criticism was deeper than it had ever been and concentrated on the concept of humanity (jen). This concept is the core of Confucian philosophy and means the relation or love between man and man. The radical Marxist critic uses the theory of class division as the framework for his criticism of Confucius.

The critic says that such human relations are only applicable to the members of the ruling class, but never apply to the common people. *Analects* 14:6 is taken as an example: 'The Master said, "We may take it that there are cases of gentlemen who are unbenevolent, but there is no such thing as a small man who is, at the same time, benevolent."'[13] Traditional scholars would understand that the distinction between gentlemen and mean men lies in moral qualities, not social class; in the Communists' view both the thinker and the morality are inevitably affected by class interest.

After decades of criticism and reassessment, modernists have all agreed on one point, namely there is no Confucian solution to China's problem. A break with the past has to be made and in a clear-cut manner. They have also agreed that only science and democracy can save China. To translate these two words into action has meant replacing the classical curriculum by science and scientism in education and in Chinese thought and abolishing traditional institutions of Chinese society. However, as to the interpretation of science and democracy, modernists have disagreed among themselves on ideological grounds.[14] Nevertheless, the break with tradition and the belief in science and democracy became focal points for debate between traditionalists and revolutionaries.

CONFUCIAN REACTIONS

The emphasis on science by the modernists led to a great controversy between science and philosophy. The spokesman from the traditional side was Carsun Chang (1889–1969). He cautioned people not to exaggerate science as omnipotent and capable of solving all problems. He pointed out five basic differences between science and a philosophy of life. 1 / A philosophy of life is always subjective, while science is objective. When a topic is subjective, various and conflicting views and experiences can be expressed, yet no experiment can be conducted in order to determine which one of them is right. 2 / Science is controlled by logical method and restricted by system, while philosophy arises from intuition. Philosophical views do not necessarily depend on logical formula and are not governed by definitions or method; they depend on the thinkers' conscience and hence are intuitive. 3 / In contrast to the analytical method of scientific inquiry, the process of philosophy usually involves synthesis. As the latter includes all or a number of items related to life, any isolated analysis would be meaningless. 4 / Science is subject to the law of cause and effect; because the law is mechanical it can be manipulated by another master agent, namely man. A philosophy of life and its practical implications, such as confession and self-education, are all determined by man's free will and are entirely controlled by man himself; apart from him there is no other master agent. 5 / Science, based on natural phenomena, classifies objects for the purpose of discovering their similarities. Consequently, the principle behind these similarities is sought. Human beings are different in ability and in temperament. They are distinguished from things through their reason as well as their emotions. Because of these fundamental differences, the traditional philosopher concludes that 'the solution of problems pertaining to a philosophy of life cannot be achieved by science.'[15]

A more systematic critic of modernity from a Confucian viewpoint is Liang Shu-ming, who has gone further than the other Confucian critics.[16] To Liang, science and technology are not only incapable of solving philosophical problems, but are also not a dynamic force for man's transformation. It is not science but culture and philosophy that determine civilizations. He classifies the pattern of world civilization and its philosophical root into three ways: Western, Chinese, and Indian. Western culture, with its philosophy of progress which comprises the conquest of nature for material gains, gives more attention to scientific knowledge and is positive in its outlook. Its principal aim is to solve problems between man and nature to the advantage of man. Chinese culture comes next, as one of moderation and harmony. It is not aimed at the conquest and manipulation of nature to satisfy the material life of man and is not interested in pure scientific knowledge. Its purpose is to teach man how to live harmoniously with other people and with himself. It seeks primarily to solve the problems between man and man. Indian culture is the third way, going retrogressively in ideas and desires, with self-restraint as the key. The Indian way concentrates on solving the problems between man and his soul.

Liang uses the terms 'progress' and 'retrogressive' not as value judgments but descriptively. He considers each of these ways to provide a solution to man's needs at different stages. The modern culture of material satisfaction is necessary at the moment as it leads to a life of abundance. When man came from pre-modern poverty, material plentifulness was absolutely necessary. However, without a happy relationship between man and man, merely material satisfaction cannot solve the problems of life, because struggle, fighting, and conquest make man's life miserable. Under these circumstances Confucian philosophy becomes a suitable means to help man. A combination of material well-being and a harmonious relation between men will lead men into a new, rich, and happy society. When man has plenty to eat, plenty to wear, and a good dwelling, and when he is harmonious with his fellow men, he may proceed to the Indian way, to deal with the problem of his soul.

Confucian philosophy is based on the Chinese metaphysic that considers life to be right and good. Confucius repeatedly glorified life. He said: 'The great characteristic of Heaven and Earth is to produce.'[17] The Confucian school also states: 'What Heaven imparts to man is called human nature. To follow our nature is called the Tao.'[18] Life is sacred in origin, and to follow its sacred nature is the way. Because of worldly attractions, man is capable of swaying away from his nature when he is deluded by worldly desires. At the economic level there is a conflict between righteousness and profit. Righteousness originates from the Tao, and profit is developed from desire. Confucian tradition is not against profit, but considers it as secondary and subject to righteousness. From this viewpoint the Confucian critic sees the evil of modern economy in the form of free enterprise. It places profit as the chief motivation and leads to a massive mechanical production that concentrates on profit but not distribution. As a result, some painful and abnormal phenomena prevail, for example, mass unemployment amid over-production, and poverty amid plenty. From a philosophical perspective, this situation does not give life, but harms life. When one examines the gains and the losses of science and technology as a whole, the conclusion is obvious.

This contrast is also reflected in social and cultural characteristics. Liang classifies Western society as individualistic or socialistic in contrast to Chinese society, which he describes as basically ethical. He considers that this basic difference makes the Western form of modernity unsuited to Chinese needs. He thinks that the church has been the core of Western tradition, organizing and leading people in their actions. This structure is reflected in the political system as well as in the productive mode. Family plays only a secondary role in the society, and even more so in our time. In contrast, Chinese society is ethically centred and the family is its basis. Mutual affection, co-operation, and harmony are the ideals of Chinese life, while competition and conflict between individuals or groups are characteristic of Western society. Liang considers that the Confucian concept of social culture made Chinese society free of class conflict. There existed no oppressive landlords and no antagonistic divisions between capitalists and labourers. He concedes there are divisions in Chinese society, but they are not antagonistic in character. His view of China's situation renders meaningless the Marxist theory of class struggle through violence, as there exist neither classes nor antagonistic divisions in the country.

Liang's understanding of Chinese culture and society makes his criticism of the socialist form of modernity obvious. He challenged the universality of Marxism by pointing out its inapplicability to Chinese culture and social structure. His denial of class antagonism in Chinese tradition challenged the Marxist assertion of human history as a history of class struggle. His contention that Chinese society was agrarian led him to think that there was no social base for a revolution, i.e. industrial labour forces. His trust in family affection led him to support Kropotkin's theory of mutual aid, which conflicts with Marxist theory of class hatred. His view of Chinese society as free from the antagonism of class conflict denied the Marxist theory of dialectical change through revolution.

For similar reasons Liang and some other Confucian critics generally consider the democratic system to be equally unsuitable for China. Democracy, they say, is a system in which the majority rules but in the Chinese situation the majority is silent and apathetic in politics. They point out that when the Chinese intellectuals were crying out for democracy in the early decade of the present century their number was less than one-hundredth of one per cent. The Chinese of that period, they continue, were apathetic to the democratic movement because they were busy in the struggle to remain alive and could not afford the time and energy for political discussion or action. In their view democracy requires a free competition among political parties, through their platforms. For this there must be a communication system or systems so that the political plans can reach the people. Literacy is another prerequisite, so that people can read about a political argument. However, the Confucian critics contend, neither of these prerequisites is met by China as there is no mass communication system and most people cannot read or understand conflicting arguments put forward by political parties.

Apart from these practical considerations Liang believed that philosophy and culture determine the pattern of a nation, and that the rest is secondary. Under these circumstances, the Confucian philosophy of self-contentment and self-restraint should be highly valued as they can help to correct some of the excesses of modern life. For example, a democratic competition requires an election campaign in which the candidates glorify themselves. This practice of self-glorification stands exactly opposed to the Chinese 'virtue' of modesty, which considers boasting and the criticizing of others as wrong. Inner conflict, mutual checking, and mutual supervision form the dialectical procession in the Western system through which outward achievement may be accomplished. Confucian virtues are in diametrical contrast to this spirit; mutual trust and mutual respect are the key in the tradition.

THE DILEMMA

The modernist attack on Confucian tradition has hit at its weaknesses effectively. Confucian tradition is a product of feudal China. The lack of pure philosophy made the tradition difficult to separate from its historical setting. Social and political institutions created during two thousand years, in the name of Confucianism, tied the tradition to corruption and bureaucracy; practical philosophy often becomes entangled with old social structures that protect the privileged few. A humanistic teaching, Confucianism lays stress more on the relationship between man and man than on that between man and nature. In an age when population pressure and popular expectations are so great, the gentle ways of love and respect have become almost meaningless. Then, too, there are currently some bureaucrats in Taiwan and Hong Kong who still talk about Confucian virtues, but act otherwise. This social and cultural background provides more ammunition to the modernists in their anti-traditional movement. These are the reasons why Confucian apologists have been unable to check the rush of China toward modernity.

Modernists were able to overcome Confucian objections and push the country and its culture into the 'new age.' Yet the Confucian cautions and criticisms still seem valid. Modernity may bring plenty to the Chinese, though no one knows how long the process will take. Long before material well-being is attained, harmony and happiness seem already lost. Various kinds and degrees of sufferings are the price paid by the Chinese for a dream that still seems too remote to be realized. Individual freedom and socio-economical equality, which the modernist advocated at the beginning of the century, look like a bad joke among Chinese intellectuals. The breakdown of family life has made people lonely, with nothing to rely on, and has increased anxiety. The lack of moderation has led the country into bloody clashes.

When one looks at how both sides, Confucian traditionalists and modernists, are able to point out each other's weaknesses and yet are unable to overcome their own defects, one sees the dilemma of China and of modern man at large. Man cannot return to the past and 'the good old days' and is not courageous enough to give up modern comfort and facilities. At the same time, the new age proves to be neither perfect nor satisfying. We are on a road of confusion. Neither past nor present contents us, and the future seems even more gloomy because of the disappointments of the present.

What will we do in this dilemma? One helpful sign is that the limitations of both tradition and modernity have become clear. The hope of retaining the past is a delusion; the dream of a new society is shattered. When the delusion and the dream are gone, we are forced to wake up and face our difficulties. But with an awakening can come hope. What we need is deliberate and forceful thought.

NOTES

1 See Hu Shih Our Attitude toward Modern Western Civilization' trans W.T. Chan in W. Theodore de Bary et al *Sources of Chinese Tradition* II (New York: Columbia University Press 1967) 191ff.

2 Quoted from a translation of Mao Tse-tung's words, in D.W.Y. Kwok *Scientism in Chinese Thought 1900–1950* (New Haven: Yale University Press 1965) 19

3 This essay has been translated and published in de Bary *Sources* 153ff. For Ch'en's career and his critique of traditional Chinese civilization, see Kwok *Scientism* 45ff, and Chow Tse-tsung *The May Fourth Movement* (Cambridge, M A: Harvard University Press 1960) 302ff.

4 See *Li-chi* or *Book of Rites* 'fang-chi' sections 30 and 17. James Legge trans *Sacred Books of the East* (Oxford: Clarendon Press 1885) 295 and 290.

5 Chow Tse-tsung *May Fourth* 303ff

6 Ibid 302

7 Tsai *Chung-kuo ch'uan-t'ung ssu-hsiang tsung p'i-p'an* (reprint Shanghai: T'ang-ti ch'u pan-she 1952)

8 D.C. Lau trans *Confucius: The Analects* (Harmondsworth 1979) VIII 14, 94

9 Ibid XVI 8, 140

10 Ibid

11 Ibid XVI 1, 138

12 Trans from *Ch'un-ch'iu fan-lu* section 13, *Ssu-pu ts'ung-k'an ch'u-pien suo-pen* ed. (Shanghai: Commercial Press 1936) 29a

13 *Analects* 124

14 For the difference of ideology among modernists, see Kwok *Scientism* 20ff.

15 Chang's essay on the subject has been partially translated; see de Bary *Sources* 173–5.

16 Liang's work on the topic has been selectively translated in ibid 187–91. For a detailed study of his thought and contribution, see Guy S. Alitto *The Last Confucian: Liang Shu-ming and the Chinese Dilemma of Modernity* (Berkeley: University of California Press 1979) 82ff.

17 From the translation of Wing-tsit Chan in *A Source Book in Chinese Philosophy* (Princeton: Princeton University Press 1963) 268.

18 From 'The Doctrine of the Mean' in ibid 98

WILFRED CANTWELL SMITH

Responsibility

The modern West can be understood and therefore its problems intelligently dealt with when it is seen not only in relation to our own past but also in the context of world history generally. In this context it appears as one powerful yet rather bizarre development among human cultures. A thesis might be argued that the difference between the twentieth-century West and earlier phases of Western culture, especially the mediaeval Christian or classical era, is comparable to the difference between it and other, non-Western, civilizations.

My purpose here is not to investigate this thesis generally but to see whether it may be illustrated by selecting one particular item for consideration. The item is the issue of moral responsibility.

As one looks out over the sweep of human history on our planet thus far, one may note that among the most distinctive, powerful, and vivid of ideas has been that of a Day of Judgement. The idea has been specific, and has played a specific role in human affairs. Of course, it has varied in detail from place to place, from century to century, from village to city to aristocrat court; has been interpreted in varying fashion, and been received with a noticeable range in emphasis, literalness, and colour. Nevertheless, by calling it 'specific' I mean that, despite variations on the theme, the metaphor is readily identifiable, and once launched has been relatively constant: it arose at a specific time and place, spread over wide areas of our earth but not over others, has dominated thought, and art, and outlook, and behaviour in certain cultures and civilizations at certain times. Thus it has had a specific history, worth our pondering. So mighty a role has it played in the lives of certain societies at certain times that its demise is itself a rather monumental matter. A world-view that no longer has this erstwhile central motif is substantially different from one that has never had it. The lacuna gapes. The process of its waning is perhaps as historically consequential, as well as fascinating, as that of its one-time rise.

In the course of its long and elaborate history, the Day-of-Judgement idea has normally been associated with the notions of Heaven and Hell. They are not, however, interchangeable, nor even inseparable; and they should not be confused. Heaven and Hell constitute a considerably more widespread metaphor, one that has prevailed over larger segments not only of both time and place but also of human orientation. Geographically and chronologically the Heaven-and-Hell vista far outruns our particular theme, without in its turn having been universal: one might say that the Day-of-Judgement societies (or eras) are a sub-set of Heaven-and-Hell ones. Without making an elaborate or careful calculation, yet in a preliminary way one might hazard an estimate that well over half, but perhaps not over three-quarters, of all human beings to date have lived their lives in the light of a Heaven-and-Hell interpretation, while maybe half of these (most notably, in terms of numbers, the Islamic and Christian movements, the world's two largest communities to date; but not, as we shall presently consider, India and China) have, further, seen the universe in a Day-of-Judgement framework.

The difference is also, however, cultural. Heaven-and-Hell is a metaphysical or cosmological/ontological apprehension, and need not have, or anyway stress, dynamic or historicist dimensions; whereas a Day-of-Judgement motif is eschatological, and has characterized those outlooks whose apprehension of reality is in terms of movement and purpose, is of an historical process that is ultimately significant, is going somewhere, for whom tomorrow tends to be more important than yesterday, and for whom will is central.

There is a further point, that while the Heaven-and-Hell themes tend no doubt towards a dualistic outlook, yet overall that link has in fact been less close, historically, than one might have expected; whereas the Day-of-Judgement theme converges quite markedly with the either/or dichotomizing spirit, which has characterized much of the northern and Western quarter of our planet, and is most pronounced in what I have elsewhere called Persian conflict dualism. (This last is to be distinguished not only from monisms of various kinds and pluralisms, but also from, for instance, the complementarity dualism of Chinese Yin-Yang. It includes also the true-false polarity in the current phase of the history of Western thought and logic.)

The Day-of-Judgement theme seems to have been formulated in the Near East, about the middle of the first millennium BC, most eloquently and effectively by the Iranian prophet Zarathushtra, and to have spread then relatively quickly to surrounding cultures, one or two of which picked it up and in turn then gradually disseminated it throughout Europe, super-Saharan Africa, and half of Asia. It is virtually unknown to the Old Testament, but had begun to shape Jewish thought before the time of the New, and is given its perhaps most dramatic and explosively powerful presentation in the Qur'an. The Jewish, Christian, and Islamic movements and the civilizations built by and around these have been the three chief branches of this mighty human vision. The Zarathushtrian (in India, now, Parsi) movement is another, smaller, one. Of course, boundaries have not been clear or firm, either in time or space.

It may be noticed that I have avoided the terms 'belief/believe' here, it being a subthesis of mine engaging my attention these days that this modern Western concept can obstruct or distort our understanding of other peoples and cultures. The modern notion that believing is what religious people do is inherently reductionist, I have come to see. Specifically, one may point to the stark difference, even contrast, between using terms like Heaven and Hell on one hand to denominate stupendous sectors of the universe, into one or the other of which one is about, perhaps irretrievably, to step, and the reality and permanence of which are greater than the entire historical process and the whole material world, and using them on the other hand to designate ideas in certain people's minds at given times and places here on earth. If a term such as 'belief' can harbour this massive ambivalence or ambiguity, it can serve us inadequately. This point, however, is but in passing.

The sociologist Will Herberg has remarked that for moderns, man is an organism reacting to its environment; for the Greeks, man was an intellect encased in a body; for the Judaeo-Christian tradition (and I would wish to expand this in specific ways), man is an immortal soul answerable to God for its deeds.

This brings us into the heart of our topic for discussion here. It is the word 'answerable' that constitutes the crux.

My thesis is that our Western concept of responsibility is derived from and in some sense integral with the Day-of-Judgement notion. To say, whether speaking of oneself or of one's neighbour, that one is morally responsible, means, etymologically and in some fashion residually, that one recognizes that one will one day have to answer for what one has done, and will be judged for it. Substantially, one is rewarded or penalized, or forgiven; but formally, the point is that one answers – must answer. And 'responsibility' is essentially a formal notion.

Responsibility, in this fundamental sense of being questioned as to how one has acted, and having to answer for it, can be transposed from a transcendent to a mundane level (or vice versa), so that the answering is before a tangible court or a particular person. In this empirical sense we have responsible government; or in an administrative set-up a given person is responsible to a designated official (a chairman to a dean, a dean to a president, a foreman to a supervisor, and the like) or responsible for a designated group, or a designated sector of the organization: if it turns out that the screws have not been properly tightened in an assemblage, or something has gone wrong in a procedure, or something was done well and in a praiseworthy fashion, then some one specified individual knows ahead of time that it will be he or she who must answer when questions are asked. It had been contended that to some degree the hierarchicization here involved is integral to the notion of (mundane?) responsibility; yet I wonder if that be primary. One can be responsible to without being subordinate, and responsible for without being in charge. A prime minister is responsible to parliament, and a president to the electorate, in the sense that in each case the latter passes the effective verdict; and I am responsible for proof-reading my book in the sense that I shall be blamed if readers find mistakes in spelling, or other scholars, mistakes in the page references. (Joint responsibility is possible also, in that a judgement may be passed on two or more collaborators: the publishers may share responsibility in that their reputation too may suffer.)

Moral responsibility, however, transcends this pragmatic sort; and traditionally involved a hierarchy in that creatures are subordinate to their Creator and Judge. By its being 'moral' it transcends – it is concerned not just with what we cannot get away with in practice. To act responsibly is to act in the awareness that one is ultimately answerable for all one's deeds, and not merely for those for which society has contrived or may yet contrive ways to bring one to book – or the law, or one's friends, or one's enemies. 'For the gods see everywhere,' as the poem has it, threatening those who would attend only to outward appearances or encouraging those who go beyond the utilitarian.

My suggestion, then, is that responsibility in the Western world is a concept derivative from the mighty metaphor of a cosmic Day of Judgement, that pictorialization of an event when each person will appear before the throne, to answer for his or her lifetime's deeds, and to receive an awesome verdict. This suggestion has an historical part, a contemporary part, and a more analytic or existential part. Let us consider each.

With reference to the past, I simply ask whether this is not in fact where we have got both the term and the concept. More teasing is the question for the present: whether it not be the case that the waning, or indeed the disappearance, of the Day-of-Judgement motif in our culture is correlated, and indeed inescapably correlated, with a waning sense of responsibility – and even, a waning capacity to discern what the notion might reasonably mean. This last leads us into the third facet of my question: whether the leaving behind of the Day-of-Judgement theme had not in fact left us without any intellectual content for the responsibility idea, which was once part and parcel of it. Is it theoretically possible to define responsibility in any other way?

One way of putting the issue, perhaps overly dramatizing it, might be as follows. On the one hand, I myself do not believe in life after death (the concept 'believing' is meaningful, negatively) in any literal fashion, and do not believe (again, literally) that I shall find retribution in some other world for anything that I may do or write (or think, or feel) in this. On the other hand, I do in fact use the term 'responsibility'; and I like to imagine that I am not being unduly arrogant or deluded if I even say that I live responsibly. I beg leave to be allowed

to think of myself as a fairly responsible person. My problem is
whether I am being consistent in this matter. It seems on reflection not
altogether unlikely that, at least to some degree, for persons like myself
both our conceptual use of the notion in our thinking, and our practical
use of it in our behaviour, may in reality be hang-overs from a time
when the Day of Judgement was quietly yet vividly real, and from a
society still operating in significant part under the centuries-long impact
of this powerful conceit. This is part of the more general question as to
whether perhaps all of us in a culture in decline are not living by
drawing on the capital, and not merely on the interest, of our inherited
legacy.

I do not, of course, think these questions quite unanswerable; yet
neither do I find them quite fatuous. Perhaps a more moderate way of
pointing my question would be the following. Is it part of the moral
crisis of culture in this age that we have yet to find or to forge an intellectually coherent, rationally persuasive, activatingly cogent, content for
or counterpart to the concept of responsibility bequeathed to us from
the past?

My colleague Professor Hilton Page (in an unpublished paper) has
remarked on the relatively recent currency of the actual term 'responsibility' in our language, a recency otherwise perhaps none too consonant
with my present interpretations. I find myself wondering whether it
may conceivably have something to do with the waning of the over-
arching conceptual framework for men's lives of a Day of Judgement
and of the whole Christian *Weltanschauung*, so that what was once
taken for granted – or was expressed vividly on all sides in art and
poetry and the like – came to require separate articulation. This would
be a process that is traceable often in human history; and is one to
which Chuang-tzu in particular and the Taoists gave expression in
China, averring that for a virtue to be conceptualized means that it is
already moribund, its spontaneity gone.

II

My own tentative answer to my own question would go somewhat as
follows. Such an answer has already been hinted at in my use two or

three times of the term 'metaphor.' The Day-of-Judgement notion has been one of the great human metaphors – but for what? The term 'responsible' is similarly metaphorical, indeed is derivatively so; but again, for what human quality? It is not *a priori* obvious that what men and civilizations have affirmed in metaphors and symbols over the millennia we can explicate in plain prose. Yet we can try. Or we can perhaps find or forge, to repeat that phrasing, a substitute metaphor of our own. My contention, in any case, would be that although verbally, and at a certain level of thought, the Day-of-Judgement theme and the responsibility language have served for hundreds of millions of men and women for a couple of millennia as the imaginative form on which a given moral quality was overtly dependent, nevertheless in reality, and at a deeper level, the situation was rather vice versa: the moral quality was primary; to it the imaginative form gave expression; and it sustained the symbolic picture, and the verbalization. This is how human history proceeds. Symbols, ideas, language, institutions, and the rest, elicit, nurture, and fortify human propensities, especially for the majority of us; yet despite their capacity for some independent persistence, they endure only because there is interaction between them and the persons to whom they are significant – and in the final analysis they arise in the first place, and persist, as derivative from persons. They make us, yes; but in large historical perspective, this is finally subordinate to the fact that we make them.

If my first point, then, is that the concept 'responsibility' is derivative from, and perhaps finally dependent upon, the Day-of-Judgement motif, my second point is that this motif is in its turn derivative from, and dependent upon, an inherent quality of man. It is evidence for such a quality. That quality, like other human qualities, may require symbolic expression in order to become widely evoked, rather than remaining latent, and corroborated rather than feeble, and may require conceptual expression in order to be thought about. Yet ultimately it lies within us, prior to all expression.

Our present-day task lies in this realm of articulate expression. Moderns feel that there is something human and important to which the term 'responsibility' refers, while at the same time we are not quite sure what it be. And unless we can give ourselves some account of it, symbolic or conceptual or both, the quality wanes. I will illustrate the

thesis, however, in perhaps more objective fashion, again from my his-
tory-of-religion field, by instancing the Hindu case, in what I trust may
prove an illuminating way.

Hindus have not had a Day-of-Judgement concept, have not been
eschatologically minded (nor even much, historically minded), and
strictly speaking have had no concept to which our term 'moral responsibility' is exactly applicable. Nevertheless, they have operated within a
profoundly embedded and deeply suffusing counterpart vision, to which
it is superficially, at least, legitimate, and even requisite, that a notion
of responsibility be vividly ascribed. Hindus live responsible lives as
surely as do any other people, in any but the most precise meaning of
the term. What I have called their counterpart vision, dramatic and
powerful, is their so-called 'law of *karma*.' This has hardly been a
doctrine, so much as a presupposition – in that it has underlain and
coloured all their doctrines, and most Buddhist ones too. What they
have had to say is couched in terms of answers to questions that are
formulated in the light of this way of viewing the world. They perceive
the empirical universe as operating according to two parallel and inter-
twining causal laws. According to one of these, for them (as for us)
every physical action is an item in an on-going chain of cause and
effect. The other is a law according to which, at least so far as human
life is concerned, every action is involved also in a chain of moral cause
and effect. Every good action (action in accord with *dharma*, the moral
law, or with his or her particular *dharma*) of every person has good
results for that person; every evil action has bad results. The righteous,
therefore, prosper; the wicked suffer.

Unlike similar theses that have been advanced in other cultures, this
one is totally foolproof, since the results mentioned may accrue over
more than one lifetime. Given the notion of transmigration, which goes
along with this, this conception of *karma* is beautifully worked out, is
quite invulnerable to logical or rational or moral criticism; it makes
unassailable sense. It is utterly impartial and fair, rigorously and relent-
lessly so; and utterly just, ruthlessly so. It makes the caste system, to
take that one example, vastly more egalitarian and vastly more just
than any social order that we in Western cultures have ever attained,
or in our wildest Utopias ever dreamed. If one commits a crime, for
instance, or a sin, one may not get caught in this lifetime, but will be

born, next time round, lower down the scale, or in a broken home, or with a low IQ, or will marry a recalcitrant or unfaithful wife. The point that I wish to make here, however, is that this law, so called, of *karma* is totally automatic. It is not administered by any god, it has nothing to do with rewards and punishments if these concepts are thought of as in any fashion personalized; it simply describes how things are in this universe of ours, like the law of gravity in Western physics. Religion, if we were to use that term for Indian affairs, does not preach this theory: it preaches rather how to get around it, or beyond it, as it were, by transcending the universe that inherently operates so.

Now this perception of the empirical world is quite fascinating; but I do not propose to pursue it. I simply note that it may be called a theory of moral responsibility superficially – since it affirms with unpitying force that whatsoever a man sows, that shall he also reap; superficially but not strictly, since here one does not 'answer' – to anyone or for anything. There is no judge; and no judgement. Every act simply sets in motion a chain of inescapable consequences, which are – for him or her who performs it – precisely adjusted, down to the finest detail, to the act's inherent moral quality. Now those of us who do not 'believe' (sic) this, and do not 'believe' in transmigration, simply note that there are here striking similarities to, and striking differences from, the comparable but disparate Day-of-Judgement motif. Both are imaginative. Neither is persuasive to outsiders. Yet both are evidence, especially in their persistence over the centuries and over wide swaths of the globe, that humankind has an interior moral sense of which we see here two divergent, mutually incompatible, eloquent, and mighty conceptual expressions. Any interpretation of man that does not do justice to this moral sense of ours is untrue to the evidence.

Responsibility is a metaphor, in our day maybe inept, for something real in human life that we may fail to understand but cannot gainsay.

III

Just as my second point, then, enlarges and in a sense contradicts my first, so however my third enlarges and in a sense contradicts, in turn, my second. I shall set it forth, briefly, and bring this to a close. It is this: that the sense of retributive justice, whether a personal judgement or impersonal requital, in both the Jewish-Christian-Islamic and the Hindu instances, is negated, or anyway transcended, by the central message (kerygma) in each case of the various religious affirmations that have maintained this very sense. 'Salvation is by faith, not by works' is the Lutheran formula; but in variations on this theme the good news proclaimed in all these communities is precisely that the final truth of humankind is that we shall not be judged on the Day of Judgement according to our deeds, that we are not left in the bondage of karma. It is affirmed that through the death and resurrection of Christ, or through the mercy of God, or through one or another of the 'ways' of liberation (the tri-marga of moksa), or through faith (Hebrew emunah, Islamic iman), self-surrender, or whatever, one transcends that. To fail to transcend it, to fail to see that it has been and is transcended, is regarded as pitiful or obtuse.

If moral responsibility is a basic truth of human life, yet it is, the historical records suggests, a preliminary truth only, which it is the business of faith or grace or wisdom or insight to move well beyond. Human beings and various human communities have formulated the matter in what appear to be diverse ways, through a variety of symbolic forms and conceptual interpretations. None the less it has been the well nigh universal testimony of our race, certainly that of the vast majority of intelligent civilized human beings throughout world history, that the moral quality of our lives is a truth to which any sense of direct moral responsibility for our actions gives expression in a way that is a first approximation only, pitiably narrow and even, ultimately, blind.

May we conclude with a question, which might take perhaps this form, once one has surveyed the matter in the perspective of world history. Is it the case that 'responsibility' as a concept is a legitimate and forceful, but not a requisite, metaphor to express a fundamental truth of our life on earth, below which it is, to put it mildly, neither reasonable nor good to fall, yet above which it is not merely reasonable and good, but indeed wise and probably even necessary, to rise?

Irresponsibility is hopelessly bad; but responsibility is, at best, inadequately good.

Might one go further and ask: Is it perhaps the inability of our modern culture grandly to rise above this level that accounts for the widespread propensity to fall below? Is it perhaps the case that a failure to transcend the moral works itself out as a failure even to attain it?

TERENCE PENELHUM

Faith, reason, and secularity

The secularity of our age has been the subject of much comment. However we define the concept of secularity, it is a truism, even a tautology, that the process of secularization is a process of decline in the influence of the dominant religious tradition of a culture. Since religious traditions vary, understanding secularization in a particular culture requires understanding the decline of the specific religious tradition dominant in it. In our own case this is, of course, Christianity.

The first step, therefore, in reaching an understanding of the secularization of our culture must be that of offering a partial characterization of how the world looks to someone who sees it in the context of a Christian faith. Such a characterization is itself religiously neutral. It should be reached independently of trying to persuade anyone that this way of viewing the world is right or wrong. If this can be done successfully, the next step is to give a partial description of the change in world-view involved in the transition to a secularized state of mind, and some indication of what has brought it about.

In this essay I shall attempt these two tasks and then try to indicate how far philosophical thought can go in bridging the great gulf that separates the Christian and secular views of our world. In conclusion, I will offer a few considerations on how someone confronting this predicament seriously should proceed in trying to solve it in his or her own case.

I

What would our world be like if the central tenets of Christianity were true? The classic statement of them is the Apostles' Creed, which begins, 'I believe in God, the Father Almighty, Maker of Heaven and Earth.' What would the world be like if it were created by someone appropriately called 'God, the Father Almighty'?

The question might seem ambiguous. Those who do not subscribe to the Apostles' Creed are very likely to say that a world created by such a being would be very different from the way our world is – much pleasanter, perhaps, or more obviously improving as history progresses. But to understand the Christian view of the world we must recognize that it applies to the actual world that the Christian and the non-Christian share. So we are not trying to imagine what sort of world a creator properly described by our own private standards as an Almighty Father would create; rather we are trying to imagine what is involved in seeing this world as one that an Almighty Father has created.

These preliminaries suggest that to imagine the world as being the creation of God, the Father Almighty, is not to imagine it as different from the way it is when we look at it ordinarily. It is rather to add certain interpretations of it that we may not ordinarily use. Everything becomes not other than what it familiarly is, but rather what it familiarly is, and more besides. What more? The notion of creation suggests to some the sort of thing that artists do, in moulding and manipulating material that they find and making something aesthetically satisfying out of it. Although too limited, this notion catches some of the Christian idea of Creation. Using it as far as we can, we can say that natural objects that are aesthetically satisfying to contemplate (flowers, mountains, sunsets) have their pleasing configurations because they have been put together by God's design, somewhat as aesthetically pleasing artefacts are put together by human design. To imagine this is not to imagine that the botanists and the geologists and the meteorologists have made errors in their descriptions of how these phenomena come to be: only that God puts these pleasing results together via the natural processes that they describe. Hence these processes are whatever the botanist and the geologist and the meteorologist say that they are, and more besides.

The idea of Creation is not the same, through and through, as the idea of the artistic assembling of materials. The artist finds his materials; he is restricted by their limitations; and he is himself limited in his ability to plan what to do with them and to control them so that his intentions can be realized. The doctrine of Creation is one in which God is free of all these limitations. Some of the implications of this can be understood if we recall Genesis: 'God said, "Let there be light"; and there was light.' The fact that in this story there was light before there was a sun may indicate that the story is mythical and not a piece of literally true history. But this does not hinder us from understanding the idea of Creation expressed within it. If anything, it helps. A natural phenomenon comes to be merely and only because God wills that it should be. God does not have to create a luminary object first in order to get light afterwards. He might do that; but he does not have to. If he chooses that light should come into the world by means of the sun, then he wills that the sun should come into being first, and the light next. But then he wills the whole sequence. He does not need to have the sun there first if he does not wish to. The sequences that we find are sequences that he chooses should be there in that order, but each part is the outcome of his willing it to be so and requires nothing more.

So we must add to our imaginative exercise the fundamentally important thought that all natural events and processes are the result of divine decision and that that decision alone is enough to produce them. And without that decision they would not happen. Of course the decision and the event do not have to occur together. God is Creator: so if he wills in 2,000,000 BC that the sun will set in Alberta at 4:32 pm MST on 1 January 1978 AD, then that is enough: it will set exactly then. He has, in 2,000,000 BC, done all that is needed. So what we observe at this time is whatever God wills should be at this time; we do not know and we need not care when he wills it. We do not determine these natural phenomena; we only find them. We sometimes put this by describing the phenomena as data, things that are given. That is what the Creed says that they are; they are given, in both senses.

There is a danger in the language so far used. It suggests that each event is somehow thought up separately by God, and this in turn suggests that the whole sequence of natural events is to us arbitrary and unpredictable. We know that this is not so. We know that natural phenomena are for the most part quite predictable because they succeed one another in regular sequences. So what the doctrine of Creation implies is that God has decided to give them to us in this regular and sequential way.

Because the world is predictable in this way we are able to change the course of it to some degree. We are aware that we have a real, but a limited, freedom of action. If there is somewhere I want to be, I can go there; I cannot be there by wishing to be but I can get in my car and drive there. My car is a machine that men have built, but they have had to build it with material that they have had to find and according to principles that they have had to discover. The materials and the laws involved represent both the limitations that men must labour under and the opportunity that men have to affect the course of nature. If the materials and the laws are products of the will of God, then when a man does something using the materials and the laws (and he can do nothing at all otherwise) he is quite literally co-operating with the will of God and God with him. And if his purposes are evil, as they often are, then God is permitting him to act out his evil choices, and this has to mean that God is literally co-operating with those choices and not frustrating them.

As a simple illustration, after the Battle of Badr, in 624 AD, the first major Muslim victory in war, the prophet Muhammad received a revelation. The revelation insisted that it was not the Muslims themselves who deserved the ultimate credit for victory, but God. For although it was the Muslims who aimed and released the arrows, it was God who carried those arrows through the air to their targets. Anyone believing, as Jews, Christians, and Muslims all do, in this dependence of man upon God has to follow the lead of this example. However free I am in my choices, the exercise of them inevitably requires the co-operation of God. And this co-operation has to be exercised even when my choice is evil or stupid, otherwise my freedom and responsibility would be unreal. If I mis-aim the arrow, then God will carry it to the place I mis-aim it at. He does not have to. But he does. This is the inevitable consequence of the fact, if it is one, that I am to some degree a free agent, in a world that depends totally on him.

So much for the dependence of the world on God. But to see familiar phenomena as dependent on God is to think about God as well as about them. The idea of dependence is incomplete without some idea, along with it, of the being on which things are alleged to be dependent. The Creed calls him the Father Almighty. The idea of Fatherhood is of course a metaphor; God is not literally our father. The metaphor is supposed to convey a picture of the sort of person that the creator is. He is a person who, in addition to the power that enables him to create, is also a source of care, protection, and moral guidance. In this notion of Fatherhood we find the classic expression of all these personal aspects of the deity, which are intended to soften the otherwise frightening impact of the picture of the creator as all-powerful and all-dominant. For if the all-powerful creator is also one who cares for the creatures he has brought into existence, if that is why he keeps them in existence (and not because he wants them to amuse him, for example), then a sense of dependence ought not to inspire terror and anxiety, but to remove terror and anxiety. This does not necessarily mean that we are going to have a pleasant time of it, merely that we ought not to be afraid or anxious if we do not have a pleasant time of it. The image of fatherhood is protective, but it is not supposed to be soothing. It is a rigorous notion. We are supposed to remain free of anxiety and fear, but that does not mean that the world will not contain within it phenomena which, without the interpretation that an Almighty Father lies behind them, it would be entirely reasonable to fear. A father protects one from real dangers, not just imaginary ones. He also gives moral guidance. To give someone moral guidance is not to make his decisions for him. If this is the correct characterization of the sort of being that we all depend on, we would expect to find that he has provided general indications of how we should behave, but that even with the best of intentions we will sometimes find it difficult to decide what to do in specific situations and will have to think it out for ourselves. We should also expect to find that, as free agents, his children will often not do what he says they should do and will use the creative power he places in their hands in ways that spoil the world he has created for them.

These observations are not meant to solve the traditional problem of evil; rather they show what the world looks like to someone who thinks it has been created by an Almighty Father. Unlike earthly fathers, an Almighty Father has ultimate control over all the circumstances in which he brings us up and from which he protects us. But to describe him in spite of this as Father and not only as Almighty is to imply that the evils of the world in which he places us are either there as background conditions of the sort of moral responses that he wishes us to make (for even an Almighty Father cannot place us in situations where we can respond with courage or patience unless there are some dangers in them), or are there because in spite of his moral advice we misuse the freedom he has given to us and do things with the world he has put us into that are contrary to his wishes. No doubt he could always repair the evils we perpetrate by simply taking over from us; but it is not the best father who does this. So a world that an Almighty Father has put us into will not be a hedonist's paradise and will often be quite disagreeable: a sort of moral gymnasium.

But the evil in our world goes much deeper than this. For anyone who sees it as the creation of an Almighty Father and sees him as making rather stringent demands upon us, the evil in it is not surprising and is very great indeed. For if I am free to act wrongly, and do, I am not only committing some moral misdeed, but I am also misusing divine gifts and disobeying divine commands. Every evil that men do is worse in the eyes of the man who believes in God than it is in the eyes of the man who does not. For every wrong-doing is also a sin. An atheist cannot be against sin, for he is not in a position to say that there is such a thing. I have said already that to the man who believes the world is created by an Almighty Father everything is what it is, and more besides; this goes for evil as well. This must now be compounded further. In a world which is predictable and intelligible to science because it is a world of regular sequences, acts I perform can be predicted to have certain effects. To take a topical example, if I throw my sewage into the river, the water can be predicted to become polluted. This is not just wrong and inconsiderate; it is also, if the world is created by an Almighty Father, a special kind of offence against him known as bad stewardship. But pollution of the water makes it harder for my successors to keep the water clean than it has been for me. The effects of my actions are passed on to others, so that they do not start from scratch, but further behind. There is in all things an inevitable end to the frontier stage, and when that end comes the whole world has lost its innocence, because evil choices have polluted the whole of it. When that stage is reached, not only is the world much inferior to the way it would be if God had not turned it over to us to mismanage, but also it becomes impossible for us and our successors to restore it, in spite of our knowledge of how bad it has become. The world is damaged beyond our capacity to repair it. A world such as that is one that contaminates all those who are born into it, so that they either settle for less than they should and become shallow apologists for the status quo, or give way to impotent rage or cynicism and abandon moral endeavour altogether.

So the very fact, if it is one, that the world is the creation of an Almighty Father, with its implications about the freedom of his creatures, makes it possible for it to reach a point of decay (or more fashionably, alienation), which can be corrected only by the Father himself interfering in it. It is the burden of the rest of the Apostles' Creed that he has done just that. It is well to comment here on the kind of interference that the picture of the Almighty Father as Creator suggests. It would have to be the sort of interference that serves to make possible the removal of the decay, or the alienation, without detracting from the continued freedom of human beings to obey God's wishes or disobey them. The basic ingredient of such interference is that it should provide reassurance. The reassurance is needed for those who wish, at least intermittently, to do the will of God, but would otherwise feel, on good grounds, that their efforts are hopeless because the evil in the world is too much for them. For this reassurance they would not need to be given miraculous powers. They would need some sign that in following the will of God they were in fact, in the long or short haul, helping to create a de-corrupted world in which God's will is obeyed universally. So even if, in the end, the restoration of the world to harmony with God were the result of a sudden transformation or cataclysm or judgment, this restoration is already beginning in their apparently futile actions. It is this sort of reassurance that is the central theme of Jesus' preaching about the Kingdom of God and is the central product of the teaching of the church about him since. And it is this reassurance that someone who takes seriously the concept of God as the Almighty Father has the logical right to expect to emerge if the picture is a true one. One of its results will be the alleviation of the anxiety that everyone who does not accept this picture has every right to feel, and no right not to feel.

So the person who commits himself to the view that our world is the creation of an Almighty Father will necessarily end up, as a simple consequence of the complexities of the notion, with a future-looking view of his world. The world's theistic religions are all eschatological religions.

The characterization just concluded has been religiously neutral. It has not been part of the argument that the Christian world-view is the true one. One comment on that is in order now, however. If the Christian view of our world were true, then the world would be just about the sort of world that, in fact, we find it is.

The same, of course, could be said for many other pictures of our world, including atheistic ones.

II

Our age is commonly said to be a secular age. More precisely, it is sometimes called post-Christian. How should this be understood?

A first step in understanding it is to qualify the earlier statement that the Christian sees the world in the same way that others see it, but as more besides. This is historically misleading. Our culture comes out of one in which, for centuries, most people did see the world in a more or less Christian way. The evolution of a secular culture has really been a process of subtraction from that composite way of viewing it. For this reason it is culturally accurate, as well as fashionable, to say that God is dead. The supernatural, or transcendent, dimension has gradually withered away, so that to more and more of us everything is merely what it is, and not more besides. When this view is the majority view, as it now is, it becomes correct to say that the Christian adds on beliefs that others do not have. It is this sort of culture that the churches now face.

Secularization has degrees. For what the Christian adds on to the common view of the world is complex, and any given person may only add, or subtract, a part of it. It can occur in a Christian setting. This is very important: secularization is not quite the same thing as religious scepticism, though of course they are closely connected. Someone who sees his experience in the Christian way, and whose attitudes are coloured by Christian interpretations of daily life and Christian expectations for the future, and who is able in consequence to be free of the anxieties that beset others is someone who has faith. Now faith notoriously has degrees, and insofar as it is weak it is primarily because the person who has it is nevertheless also partly secularized. This is very easy: even if I believe that everything is what it is and yet God's creation besides, I might become so absorbed in what it is, in those dimensions of it that I share with unbelievers, that I tend to forget that it is also God's creation and need prophetic or sacramental reminders. By the time I live through the week to Saturday evening, I need Sunday morning. And even though I might frequently remind myself that I do think of my world as God's creation, I might not derive from this the freedom from anxiety that it should give to me and allow the cares of the world to harrow me needlessly – Jesus preached against this weakness of faith in his famous utterances about the lilies of the field. And finally, I might use my conviction that the world is in God's hands as an excuse to ignore the extent to which it is alienated from God and drift in facile optimism, allowing the pleasures of the world to satisfy me too easily. Catholics have a name for this sort of believer: they call him the *pococurante*, one who cares little. So even in a Christian context, partial secularization occurs, and occurs regularly, as the devitalization of faith.

On the other side of the coin, secularization is often not complete in a sceptic. I do not think that any theological capital can be made out of this, but it is still true. It would be surprising if it were not; for something as complex and deeply rooted as Christianity can hardly be abandoned in all details in a few generations. It is easy to point here to the families who still irrationally insist on baptism and Christian burial, with no religious life in between, but there are more interesting examples of incomplete secularization than this. One of them, I think, is the extensive and interesting literature of the absurd. The world is only properly described as absurd, or lacking in meaning, if it is without some significance that by rights it ought to have. To say that it is absurd is to react to the absence of something that you think it is reasonable to expect to be there. In our culture this is to respond to the absence of the sort of meaning that Christianity has taught us is present in it. Now if Christianity is false, then one has no right to expect it to be there, and no right to cry 'Absurd' at the world that lacks it. All one is doing is shaking one's fist at the empty sky. As secularization advances, the sense of absurdity can be expected to pass, and is already beginning to do so.

So it is misleading to oppose faith and secularity in a manner that implies a given person must be an example of the one or of the other, but cannot show traces of both. Each has gradations of purity, and each can be pursued as an ideal by the person who manifests it. It has long been familiar to the man of faith (even though most standard theological analyses of faith do not allow for it) that one of the very signs of the presence of faith in a person is his consciousness that his faith is not deep enough and needs to be intensified. The same phenomenon is characteristic of the self-consciously secular person who wishes very deeply to remove embarrassing traces of religiousness from his thought-processes. Each will try to intensify his stance by fending off the inclinations he has to manifest the stance of the other.

But having said this, let us also recognize, unambiguously, that in our own day secularization is more widespread, and more complete in those who manifest it, than at any time in the history of our culture. The sources of this fact are various, and it is quite beyond the scope of one essay to explore all of them. Two seem to be paramount. The first is the dramatic and explosive growth of scientific understanding in modern times. The second is the separation of morality from its religious ancestry. Because of the former, men are confident that they can understand their world without reference to God. Because of the latter they are confident that they can make their decisions without reference to him.

While the secularization of our culture is indeed due largely to science, it is not due to the details of science. And it is not due to the fact that science has reduced belief in magic, for one can easily believe in magic without believing in God. It is due to the progressive realization that science is autonomous. The autonomy of science means that theological notions have no place in a scientific treatise, and that it would now be regarded as intolerable in educated circles ever to suggest that the fate of a scientific theory could depend on the truth or falsity of some religious doctrine. Ever since the Holy See made its appalling tactical blunder of condemning Galileo for holding a scientific doctrine that was judged to contravene Scripture, the primary prerequisite of every theory of the relationship between scientific and religious knowledge has been that it should make it theoretically impossible for a cleric ever to have the right to reject scientific arguments on theological grounds. The only way of guaranteeing this result in advance of knowing what scientific arguments are coming up is to decide ahead of time that whatever they are they can have no bearing, positive or negative, on Christian doctrines. But once you say this you imply that no scientific statement can lead to any religious conclusion. The only way of guaranteeing that science can be left alone is to insist it has nothing of religious import to say. And this in turn means that scientific knowledge has no need to invoke religious doctrines, which can then be abandoned without scientific loss. God has been thought to have died because it has become easy to proceed as though he is intellectually unnecessary. Science has made it less common for men to add on the Christian interpretation of their common world by making it obvious to them that the addition is wholly optional. It may always have been so, but now it is obviously so.

But it is not only optional in the understanding of our world. It is also optional for us when we reflect on how to act in it. Our age is morally secular. And here the cause does not lie outside the Christian tradition, but within it.

Sceptics often talk as though Christian morality is a morality of simple obedience to divine commands. This is not so. One of the best-known passages in the Dialogues of Plato is the one where Socrates is discussing the nature of piety or holiness with the priest Euthyphro. Euthyphro represents the position that religious virtue consists in the avoidance of contamination by the meticulous practice of ritual observances. Socrates exposes the moral defects of this position by asking Euthyphro to define for him what piety or holiness is. Euthyphro says that piety is that which is pleasing to the gods. Socrates then asks him whether the actions that are called pious are so called because the gods take pleasure in them, or whether the gods take pleasure in them because they are pious acts? Behind this famous question is the view that the authority of any allegedly divine command comes from the moral correctness of what is commanded, instead of the correctness of the command being guaranteed by the statement that it comes from the gods.

The interesting thing for our present purposes, however, is that a very similar teaching is proclaimed in the New Testament by Jesus. Again and again he attacks the position which he ascribes (correctly or not) to the Pharisees that a man can ensure that he will be accounted righteous by making certain that he follows the prescriptions of the Law to the last detail. Thus interpreted, the Law is only secondarily a set of moral demands; it appears primarily as a protection for the members of the Nation to whom it has been given. One's only moral problem becomes that of subsuming new situations under the old Law, a practice known as 'building a fence around the Torah.' In the face of this Jesus insists that moral action is not a mode of self-protection, but an open-ended risk; and one of its risks is that you cannot read off detailed answers to your individual moral dilemmas from previously existing commandments. On the contrary: you have to be prepared even to find that the Law that God gave to his people can on occasion be violated in the light of your obvious moral obligations. Once this is admitted, it becomes clear that it is your duty as a potential citizen of the Kingdom of God to use your own moral judgment. Of course, what you are trying to discover is what God's will is; but in the last resort you have to use your own moral judgment to decide what it is. This is one of the sources of the infuriating vagueness of the New Testament on questions such as war or divorce. Why doesn't he come out and say whether divorce is permissible? What's the use of telling us that those whom God has put together no man should put asunder? Whom has God put together? When you know the answer to that question you already know what should be done; but that is the moral problem that you have to solve. There are general guidelines (something, incidentally, that even Socrates sometimes agreed were necessary for enlightened conduct), but they are not to be applied uncritically.

Given this insistence by the founder of Christianity on moral autonomy and responsibility as a religious duty, we can say that right at the
heart of the Christian tradition is one of the sources of the secularization of Western culture. For Christianity teaches the need for every
man to use his own moral judgment even in the application of rules
that are thought to have a religious source.

The individual's autonomy of moral decision is stressed even more
than this, however. It is not merely that Jesus teaches that one has to
use one's own powers of moral discernment to decide what God commands for us and what he does not. For our conduct to be acceptable
in God's sight it is not even necessary that we should think of our
actions in the context of God's commands at all. This is surely part of
the moral of the famous passage about the sheep and the goats. In this
story those who are judged to be righteous at the end are said to have
shown charity toward God himself; they protest that they are unaware
of ever having done so, and the reply is that they have done this to
God inasmuch as they have done it to his children. The natural reading
of this is that you can do God's will, and be counted as having done it,
without having done it as God's will. You can be deemed to have
served God's purposes merely by acting toward his children in the ways
that are dictated by your own recognition of their needs. This is a very
natural consequence of the use of the image of God as Father; for the
father who wishes for the good of his children will presumably be content when others do things for their own good, without worrying
unduly if they do not do this because of whose children they are.

With these inner springs toward an insistence on moral autonomy,
Christianity contains within it a major thrust toward the secularization
of its moral teachings. For the natural conclusion to draw is that even
though the Christian ethic does consist of the moral expression of the
will of God, the recognition of this is logically incidental to the recognition of one's moral duties to others. If one adds on to this the colossal
cultural success of Christianity in Western culture after the first years
of persecution, a success that has meant that more and more Christian
moral ideals have been accepted into the conventional wisdom of
Europe and America, there is no mystery at all about the fact that
thousands who have more or less Christian moral principles succeed in

doing so without having any more than the dimmest awareness of other Christian teachings.

III

So much for the partial account of the differences between Christian man and secular man, and how they came to be. To clarify these two outlooks is to engage in philosophical analysis. Such analysis is, in principle, neutral between the stances it tries to illuminate. Philosophy has made too much of its neutrality in recent years, and its practitioners are reminded, often heatedly, that it has traditionally not been neutral at all. What in fact can a philosopher do to assist the rational concerned contemporary to choose between the two outlooks, in addition to making them clearer to him than they may have been before?

Let us begin by asking what philosophers who have not been neutral have tried to do and what the critics of philosophical neutrality wish them still to do. They have tried to show that the choice of one of the two alternatives is rationally compelling. They have tried to show this by proving that God exists, or by proving that he does not; or by arguing that it is far more probable that he does exist than that he does not, or that it is far more probable that he does not exist than that he does. These arguments have not been successful on either side. Even if this judgment is correct it does not show that God's existence cannot be proved, or that his non-existence cannot be proved. One day someone may do one or the other. It does, however, suggest grounds for being doubtful whether either is possible. If neither seems possible, then it would seem that neither side can show the other side to be irrational to take the position it does. Each, then, is reasonable – in the minimal sense of 'not unreasonable.'

We can go further than this, however. Each side has ample resources to deflect the criticisms made by the other, and the deadlock between them is complete. The point may be illustrated.

1 / The unbeliever has the simpler position. Instead of saying that everything is what it is and more, he says that everything is what it is and no more. This view makes for a simpler world picture. Now it is a well-known feature of scientific argument that simpler theories are to

be preferred to more complicated ones if other things are equal. So
unbelief might seem to have one of the most familiar canons of rational
argument on its side. But it is easy to see the believer's rejoinder: that a
canon that is appropriate and successful in the scientific understanding
of our world is one that it is question-begging to insist upon when rais-
ing the very question of whether this world is all there is. If you do not
assume this, the argument continues, you do indeed sacrifice simplicity,
but what you lose in simplicity you gain in depth. This is surely a
stalemate.

2 / Believers will often point to alleged historical events, or docu-
ments, or persons, and say that these are revelations of God. Now a
revelation, if there are such things, is presumably something that
enables one to come to have some knowledge of God. Such an event,
or document, or person, whether it be thus revelatory or not, is an
event or document or person in the common world which the believer
shares with the unbeliever. As soon as we see this, however, we can
see that it is never unreasonable for the unbeliever to say that that is
all it is, and that it is just a historical event or personality that has natural causes and no more. So even if it is revelatory, it is not irrational
for the unbeliever to deny that it is. He does not have to deny it happens, only to insist that the natural causes producing it exhaust its significance. Again, we have a stalemate.

3 / Finally, believers often accuse unbelievers of wilful blindness. On
their terms, the charge is often justified. For unbelievers will often refuse to listen to preachers. To the believer a preacher, if he knows his
business, is someone whose task it is to present the Christian picture of
our world and our condition, so that the hearer can see that our world
is the creation of an Almighty Father. Not to listen is to ignore evidence; to ignore evidence is irrational obstinacy. However, the unbeliever will consider that what the believer sees as the presentation of
evidence is merely a set of disreputable persuasive devices – after all,
truth comes (does it not?) from the objective consideration of hard data
by men with clear heads and full stomachs and white coats. You cannot attain the truth in situations where someone is hypnotizing a captive audience softened by hymns and unnerved by feelings of guilt.
The only wise thing to do is to stay away.

These are random illustrations of the rational deadlock that exists between the two sides. Philosophy cannot resolve it, even though philosophy can clarify it and help each side to understand itself and the other better. Philosophy can be the handmaiden of theology, but also of atheism.

IV

Christian faith and secular unbelief can confront each other with each side remaining confident of the reasonableness of its own position, and having excellent internal resources for explaining in its own terms why the other side responds in the way that it does. There are no agreed neutral standards that can be used to settle the dispute between them. This estimate of the relationship between faith and unbelief is, in the traditional technical sense, a sceptical assessment of it.

The classical sceptic had a recommendation attached to such estimates of philosophical disputes: that the wise man would suspend judgment and calmly accept the inadequacy of the human intellect to probe the secrets of the universe. But we have learned from 'existential' thinkers, at least since Pascal, that whatever reason's incapacities may be, this non-commitment is not an open option for us. For not deciding is equivalent to deciding for unbelief. Agnosticism is merely atheism wrapped in mock humility. One cannot not choose.

Must one then leap wildly, without rational ground? The cult of the arbitrary choice is repulsive, especially to the philosopher; and there is in any case something odd in the suggestion that a choice that can be made in very full knowledge of the details and consequences of the competing alternatives would be irrational nevertheless. But these considerations are not decisive. The best that a philosopher, as opposed to the evangelist or the secularizer, can do is attempt to change the plane on which discussion has proceeded, in the hope that rational standards can be brought to bear in different ways. The comments that follow, which do not all lean in one direction, are offered as beginnings to such debate.

In respect to the secularization of morality, we saw that the seeds of it can be found in some of the sayings of the founder of Christianity himself, and in the widespread acceptance of Christian moral insights by secular men, who have managed to detach them from their source. So we have a world in which men of opposite religious persuasions share a common fund of moral agreement.

But even though a Christian and an unbeliever may very largely agree about the major moral issues of their time, there is bound to be a deep difference between their practical attitudes – unless the Christian is more secularized in his emotions than he thinks he is. I have already referred to the base of this difference: the Christian, though he shares the common world with others, sees it, and himself, as sustained by God and looks to a future under the reign of God to which his puny efforts now are small contributions. The unbeliever cannot share this attitude. On the contrary, he has to restrict himself to the secular dimensions and effects of his actions. This division is compatible with the two of them agreeing, to the last detail, on what should be done. What has to differ is not what they think is right, but the manner in which they can set about doing it. The Christian can be freer of anxiety, because he can (or should) be totally confident of the ultimate outcome, whatever happens in the short term. One often hears men speak with throbbing confidence of the ultimate victory of their moral cause: in the end they will overcome. Whatever makes them say so? History rather suggests that in obvious human terms sometimes one does and sometimes one does not. But in the end, if God exists, then *he* will overcome. This confidence provides an element of hope or reassurance that others are not entitled to feel. But what an enormous motivating difference this reassurance provides! It is an antidote to the sort of despair that makes most people abandon causes, and an antidote to the sort of fanaticism that makes one feel that one's own moral efforts are supremely important and must not on any account be frustrated.

One of the most difficult tasks of interpretation of the New Testament has been that of trying to infer from it some general guide to political decision-making. The task is virtually impossible. One often hears nowadays that Jesus was a rebel. He clearly was not. He refused to allow anyone to interpret his mission as one involving political action, the ultimate refusal of which is the famous 'Render unto Caesar the things that are Caesar's and unto God the things that are God's.'

One reason that scholars often give for Jesus' apparent indifference to contemporary forms of political action is that he thought that the time between his ministry and the ultimate victory of the Kingdom of God was short, and that political decisions in the interim were of minor importance. If this view is right, it explains the absence of clear guidance on this topic for those who either do not believe in the ultimate arrival of God's Kingdom at all or, if they do, have had to defer the expectation of it. But however one reads the intentions of the historical Jesus, one can readily enough infer that whatever one feels one must do politically here and now (and the text does say that Caesar, who symbolizes politics, has his due), it is not of ultimate or decisive importance; that if it fails as a moral weapon, the matter has not ended, and God is not defeated. Such an attitude is not one of indifference to politics, but one of reasonable humility about what politics can accomplish and of reassurance that all is not ultimately in vain if politics in the short run accomplishes less than we hope.

A world with a large number of moral agents with this sort of motivation and reassurance within them will, I suggest, be more morally productive than one in which moral agents have the same objectives but are without such motivation. Indeed, this view is perhaps part of what Jesus himself intended in some of his parables of the Kingdom of God and may help resolve some of the difficulties in the interpretation of his teachings about it.

But what follows? No one is entitled to such reassurance unless he believes that the Christian world-picture is true. It is natural enough, then, for someone who does not think that it is true to insist that, although it would be morally good, perhaps, if it were, it is not; so we have to do our best without it. Obviously no one ought to be expected to believe something merely because the world would be morally more productive if it were true. Truth has to come before expediency, even the loftiest sort of expediency.

This reaction may be questioned or at least circumvented. If it is true that Christianity and unbelief are both rationally defensible and a proof of either is beyond us, then perhaps there is a moral to be drawn: namely, that if one of the two views is morally better, and we are not in a position to know decisively which one is true and which false, it might be as well to choose the morally better one.

But what is meant by 'choose'? Surely not 'make oneself believe'? Perhaps not. But if this picture of the philosophical status of religious belief is correct, it would seem to suggest that the obligations to proselytize are all on one side and not on the other: that unbelievers ought to see no merit whatever in increasing their own numbers, but ought to see a good deal of moral merit in the increase of the numbers of believers.

Many doubters recognize such moral merit. If you pass any church in the city ten minutes before service-time you are likely to see cars draw up. In many of these cars there will be neatly dressed children, sometimes accompanied by their mothers; the cars will be driven by unshaven men in shirt sleeves who let their passengers off at the church door and come back for them at what they hope is the right time for the end of the service. If the sermon is longer than usual the line of cars will be round the block. Obviously what is happening here is that men who no longer believe any of this very definitely themselves still do not want to let their families grow up without it. Even though they do not quite subscribe to the view that the family that prays together stays together, they think it of some importance that some of their family should pray. Perhaps they are on to something, and perhaps this apparently inconsistent practice can be justified.

Protagoras long ago reminded us that there is a place for the application of practical standards of rationality, even where reason may otherwise seem to fail us. Such application, in one way or another, would seem clearly to favour the cause of faith. Here the lesson is similar to the one Pascal tried to teach.

But if reason fails, save on this practical level, it does so because there is no decisive ground for preferring one of our world-views to the other. This situation in turn presents a special difficulty for the believer, though it is one the magnitude of which I find it hard to assess.

If it is true that the Christian and the unbeliever share a common, scientifically ordered environment and differ not about the way in which it is ordered but about whether or not it is also the creation of an Almighty Father, then their world is one in which the belief in such a creator is optional. It is not intellectually necessary, even if it is true. But if we suppose it is true, does not this very ambiguity of the world, the very fact that it can be viewed in both these ways, become, itself, a problem? For it would surely be possible to imagine some events which, if they occurred, would remove the ambiguity – events that would render it irrational to continue to refuse to accept that the world is indeed the creation of an Almighty Father? For example, miracles. Why do they not occur in our day if Christianity is true? It is clear that if the world the believer and the unbeliever share is scientifically ordered, there could not be many miracles. For one thing, if believers thought there were many of them, they could not agree with unbelievers as they do about how the world goes usually: they would be on the look-out for strange events all the time. For another, if everyone lost their belief in scientific predictability, miracles would lose their effect.

In the first century, many people were thought to have the power to work wonders, and it was therefore possible to agree that Jesus worked miracles yet still doubt whether he had divine authority. In our non-magical world, miracles have to be very rare. But surely God could produce a judicious scattering of them? This would not be enough to break the belief in the scientific orderliness of nature, but could be just enough to bring it home to everyone that nature is not all there is.

The trouble with this wish, of course, is that if miracles are that rare, an unbeliever could always reasonably say it is doubtful that they have happened, especially if the miracles that one appeals to are supposed to have happened at a remote time in the past, so that they are known to us only from reports. This problem is notoriously the case with the New Testament miracles. It seems rational, even if it is mistaken, to say, 'Yes, if the Resurrection did happen, that proves Christian claims about Jesus to be true; but the magnitude of those claims is so great that it is not obviously necessary for me to accept them on the basis of someone else's *reports* of the Resurrection.'

To get around this one would need some indubitable sign at least in each generation. The point here is not that everyone who knew of it would then believe; merely that no one would then have any rational excuse for unbelief. There is no good theological argument to show why there should not be evidence sufficient to make it irrational: after all, it could still go on; men are free agents and can be as irrational and perverse as they like, as theologians emphasize.

If belief and unbelief are both reasonable states of mind, why does not something happen that would show unbelief to be unreasonable?

Doubters are always full of excuses and probably always would be; but why are they left with a good excuse?

One must end where one is. These considerations remain for reflection, I suggest, when the full implications of the contemporary relationship between faith and secularity are recognized. Neither looks decisive: indeed at least one of these two lines of argument must be mistaken, because either faith or unbelief must be mistaken also.

When an ambiguity such as this persists, it is natural that some will attempt to deny its presence. One form of this denial is the attempt, still popular, to secularize faith itself. No one who has followed this essay this far will be surprised by this conclusion: secularized faith is literally unthinkable.

ABRAHAM ROTSTEIN

The world upside down

For the universal and homogeneous state to be a realisable political end, Christian theism had first to be negated ... Thus the idea of the classless society, then, is a derivative of the Christian religion because modern philosophy in negating the Christian religion was aware of the truth present in that which it negated.   George Grant *Technology and Empire*[1]

I

George Grant moves among the circle of the great critics of modernity. From the vantage point of the Christian apocalypse, he attempts to come to terms with its startling recapitulation in the visions of modern secular society. Its chief embodiment perhaps is within the Marxist vision of a perfect community on earth – the universal socialist society.

Eric Voegelin is another exponent of this theme: 'For it must never be forgotten that Western society is not all modern but that modernity is a growth within it, in opposition to the classic and Christian tradition.'[2] Such a modern society precludes an effective realization of Judeo-Christian eschatology with its total reconciliation of God and man in perfect community. For Voegelin, 'the spiritual destiny of man in the Christian sense cannot be represented on earth by the power organization of a political society; it can be represented only by the church.'[3] Hence the displacement of the truths of Revelation into history is not only futile, but also culminates in the modern totalitarian experience.

Other eminent philosophers have also taken up this theme. Michael Polanyi, for example, has decreed that Marxism is a 'spurious form of moral inversion' of Christianity.[4] Within the same stream, Reinhold

Niebuhr has declared: 'Marxism is a secularized version of Christian apocalypse in which the beatitude "Blessed are the poor" becomes the basis of unqualified political and moral judgements.'[5]

There is a recurring vocabulary for this Christian critique and the terms 'negation' or 'inversion' are often used synonymously to convey the sense that the secular 'kingdom' (or, in the language of Strauss and Kojève, 'the universal and homogeneous state') is some form of mirror image of the original Christian vision.

One's vantage point in such a debate is, of course, everything. Marx himself would have found a surprisingly large area of agreement with these critics and had indeed already made use of the same vocabulary. He would, however, have been looking through the mirror from the other side. The 'Christian dialectic,' he maintained, had issued from 'an inverted world' (eine verkehrte Welt) and was thus itself 'an inverted world-consciousness' (ein verkehrtes Weltbewusstsein).[6] He claimed in fact that all ideology thus far has come to us as if it were filtered through a camera obscura, a dark room, and thus appears upside-down, standing on its head.[7] The point was, of course, as in his famous reference to Hegel, that the social world as well as its beliefs and ideologies had properly to be stood on their feet once more. Thus he would have had no difficulty in agreeing with his Christian critics that communism was a 'negation' of Christianity.

My intention here is not to obliterate the vast differences between the two camps. But an underlying question begins to force its way through. If Voegelin is correct in his panoramic view of an entity called 'Western society' with its opposing tendencies within that society, how should such a Western society be described over such vastly different millennia?

It may require an almost superhuman detachment from the long and vociferous history of internecine struggle to speak of a common tradition of belief that runs from biblical religion through Marxist eschatology. In the attempt to come to grips with some of the strikingly similar features of this tradition (without denying their overwhelming differences), I revert to the phrase 'the apocalyptic tradition.' It is a consistent tradition, the many expressions of which are characterized by a common beginning and a common end. The world is conceived initially as the home of overwhelming domination and oppression (defined in characteristically different ways). But the oppressed, in the end, are offered a vision of perfect community whether called the kingdom of God or socialism. Between the beginning and the end lies an intermediate process of transfiguration that is largely unrecognized but is shared by all the main versions of this tradition.[8] Over the three millennia from Moses to Marx, the leading actors have changed, but the basic script of the apocalyptic tradition and some of its vital vocabulary have endured.

Within the limitations of this essay, I shall touch with inordinate, if not unseemly, brevity on the Old Testament, the New Testament, Luther, Hegel, and Marx. The reader should bear in mind that there is no intention here to review their respective doctrines. Hence this is an essay neither on Revelation nor on revolution, and I shall have little to add to our knowledge of either theology or socialism.

It is an essay on the extraordinary itinerary – one might even say the 'calisthenics' – of certain types of language in the apocalyptic tradition. This interest in language is not, strictly speaking, linguistic or semantic as such. Several philosophers and social scientists hold that language is the key to consciousness and is indeed the most direct and intimate expression of it available to us. Ernst Cassirer has suggested that the mind uses words and images 'as *organs* of its own, and thereby recognizes them for what they really are: forms of its own self-revelation.'[9] The Russian psychologist Lev S. Vygotsky has come to the same conclusion from a different perspective: 'Thought and language, which reflect reality in a way different from that of perception, are the key to the nature of human consciousness.'[10]

A new and unexpected light has been thrown on this same matter by the distinguished work of Claude Lévi-Strauss. From the study of hundreds of primitive myths, Lévi-Strauss concludes that we may speak of an 'architecture of the mind.'[11] This is an arresting idea; he elaborates further that 'the unconscious activity of the mind consists in imposing forms upon content ... these forms [being] fundamentally the same for all minds.'[12] Among these forms, Lévi-Strauss throws his main emphasis on the 'universality of the binary code,'[13] that is, the inherent capacity of the mind to 'think by pairs of contraries, upwards and downwards, strong and weak, black and white.'[14] These pairs are referred to as 'chains of binary oppositions.'[15] The main process involved in the structure of myth is the setting up of contrasting pairs, the building up of a conflict, and the move toward its resolution.

To treat the apocalyptic tradition from the Bible to Marx as a system of myth does not imply an intention that is either pejorative or reductionist. The validity of the truths revealed in this tradition is not compromised by the present analysis of the medium of their articulation. But the new issue that does arise is that of the role of the human mind as a hidden but vital protagonist throughout. In this study of the myth of the apocalyptic tradition, particularly in relation to the formal rhetorical properties of the language that it employs, we are engaged in a venture not in either theology or socialism but ultimately in anthropology in its widest sense – the study of man.

II

The attempt to view the apocalyptic tradition in some overall common perspective does constitute a severe test of the reader's credulity. This challenge to the respective adherents of its various individual expressions may prove insurmountable. Yet if we are prepared to abandon, even momentarily, our fixed vantage points, a broader landscape comes into view with deep valleys as well as peaks.

Much of the drama of this tradition comes from the periodic schisms that seem virtually inherent in its existence. The New Testament grew out of the Old, Protestantism out of Catholicism, Marx out of Hegel (who maintained throughout that he was a Lutheran). One cardinal rule prevailed in the schism. The previous version of the perfect community was transfigured and negated. This negating proved to be an indispensable feature of the new starting point, that is the new version of oppressive bondage. Rosemary Reuther has pointed out that in the early Christian church 'anti-Judaism was originally more than social polemic. It was an expression of Christian self-affirmation'[16] and was closely incorporated into Christian 'antitheses' or 'negations.'[17]

The church in its turn was 'negated' in the Protestant Reformation. T.S. Eliot remarked: 'The life of Protestantism depends on the survival of that against which it protests.'

Hegel, while continually avowing his Protestant affiliation, attempted to overturn, in a gnostic fashion, the forms of self-understanding of Protestant theology. These outmoded forms, the myths, miracles, and legends, he felt, had now to be abandoned, and his own aim was to turn 'the language of religious myth into that of thought.'[18]

Marx rejected Hegel's 'dialectic of negativity' as itself too mystical. Man's bondage in history was as much to his religious self-expression as to his social institutions. Marx wished to overturn virtually all that had gone before.

Thus the great expressions of the apocalyptic tradition are necessarily as well its great schisms. It may be argued that Marx's ultimate break with any vestige of theism is the great divide in this tradition – its total secularization. Yet it grew almost 'naturally,' perhaps inevitably, out of Hegel's attempt to relocate the enduring element of Protestant truth within a gnostic, immanentist tradition. For Hegel, the self-consciousness of the individual, as well as the rule of Spirit in the universe, bore witness to the essential Christian truth.

What is so unexpected, however, is the remarkable consistency of the schismatic argument, despite the widely different contexts in which it arose. Whether one or another version of theism was at issue, or whether, as with Marx, total secularization was propounded, the mode of reasoning was always the same. On the one hand, the previous 'perfect community' had to be incorporated in the new oppressive bondage. On the other, a great deal of what had gone before was retained and reaffirmed in the new context.

Much of this inner process of schismatic articulation can be summed up in Hegel's notion of *aufheben*, with its dual connotation of 'abolishing' and 'preserving' simultaneously. This dual, antithetical process is often hidden in the English translation of *aufheben* in Hegel and Marx, where it is usually rendered simply as 'transcend.'

The first and perhaps the most dramatic instance of schism is in the New Testament. It is the model for virtually all that came afterwards. Let us first recapitulate briefly the related structure of the Old Testament. The high point of the Old Testament is the Covenant at Sinai. The rhetorical origins of the event, however, lie in Pharaoh's tyrannical domination and in the oppressive bondage of the Jews to state slavery in Egypt. The rhetoric is explicit: 'Then thou shalt say unto thy son, we were slaves unto Pharaoh in Egypt' (Deut. 6:21).

Yahweh conquers Pharaoh and replaces a tyrannical and evil lordship with an exalted lordship of justice and righteousness. The Jews in turn are transformed from oppressed slaves to Pharaoh to exalted slaves to Yahweh as in God's statement: 'For unto me the children of Israel are slaves; they are my slaves' (avadei) (Lev. 25:55). While the same Hebrew word eved is retained to connote slavery to Pharaoh as well as slavery to Yahweh, its significance has been completely inverted. In the first instance it connotes bitter overwhelming oppression, in the second instance total salvation, man's highest and most exalted vocation.

This hidden inversion of eved or slave is the precedent for other forms of inversion that constitute the route to perfect community. Another mode of inversion, for example, is used to represent the status of the 'chosen' (i.e. blessed) people: 'And the Lord shall make thee the head, and not the tail; and thou shalt be above only, and thou shalt not be beneath' (Deut. 28:13).

The Jews are now 'called by the name of the Lord' (Deut. 28:10), despite the fact that they are still his 'slaves,' and thus enter into the apocalyptic resolution of perfect community. As 'lords' they are to exist in a community of total obedience, a complementary image of the supreme Lord. At the foot of Mount Sinai, Moses relays God's promise as follows: 'Ye have seen what I did unto the Egyptians, and how I bare you on eagles' wings, and brought you unto myself. / Now therefore, if ye will obey my voice indeed, and keep my covenant, then ye shall be a peculiar treasure unto me above all people: for all the earth is mine: / And ye shall be unto me a kingdom of priests, and an holy nation' (Ex. 19:4–6). Metaphors of inversion are scattered throughout the Old Testament: 'The Lord bringeth low, and lifteth up' (1 Sam. 2:7); 'Behold the Lord maketh the earth empty and maketh it waste, and turneth it upside down' (Is. 24:1).

The New Testament follows this very same route to perfect community except for one vital change – the shift in the definition of bondage.

In place of Pharaoh, the oppressive bondage in this instance is to the body and to man's mortality. Paul refers (literally) to our 'having been enslaved under the elements of the world' (Gal. 4:3). The Greek word for 'slave,' *doulos*, is now transfigured in precisely the same way as the Hebrew *eved*. Hence the 'slaves (*douloi*) ... of sin unto death' (Rom. 6:16) become, in their inverted (exalted) status, the 'slaves of Christ' (*douloi Christou*) (Eph. 6:6).

Similarly, just as Yahweh defeats Pharaoh, so Christ abolishes death, which is 'swallowed up in victory' (I Cor. 15:54). Death's domination is inverted, and Christ brings 'immortality to light through the gospel' (II Tim. 1:10). Christians become 'heirs of God, and joint-heirs with Christ' (Rom. 8:17); the Christian is 'lord of all' (*kyrios panton*) (Gal. 4:1). This concept – 'But ye are a chosen generation, a royal priesthood, an holy nation, a peculiar people [i.e. a people for His possession]' (I Pet. 2:9) – is closely modelled on the Old Testament. This inversion from slave to lord is now the prelude to the apocalyptic resolution of the kingdom of God. Christians enter the kingdom as 'fellow-citizens with the saints and of the household of God' (Eph. 2:19).

But the schismatic character of the New Testament is highlighted as well. The oppressive bondage of the Christian is not only to man's mortality – the body, sin, and death – but also to what had gone before, the Law. The commandments and the Mosaic code had been the key to perfect community among the Jews: 'Blessed is the man ... [whose] delight is in the law of the Lord' (Ps. 1:1–2). But for Christians, 'Christ is the end of the law for righteousness to every one that believeth' (Rom. 10:4). Thus Christ 'is made, not after the law of a carnal commandment, but after the power of an endless life' (Heb. 7:16). The Law enters into the redefined realm of the Christian view of oppression. Hence (in Heb. 7:18) the commandments are 'annulled' (*aufgehoben* in Luther's translation). But the inner significance of this annulment soon becomes clear in Paul: 'Do we then make void (*heben ... auf*) the law through faith? God forbid: yea we establish the law' (Rom. 3:31). Jesus is explicit on the matter: 'Think not that I am come to destroy the law, or the prophets: I am not come to destroy but to fulfil' (Matt. 5:17).

The complaints of the Jews were vociferous. After Paul had preached his revolutionary doctrine for three sabbath days in the synagogue at

Thessalonica, the Jews made representations to the local authorities: 'These that have turned the world upside down are come hither also' (Acts 17:6). 'The world upside down' was a metaphor that was to be re-echoed in various ways in all the schismatic battles of the apocalyptic tradition we are considering, whether by the theistic or the secular tradition. It was to reappear as a casual figure of speech, a metaphor for an oppressed world, as well as a metaphor for revolution. With Luther and Hegel it reached its highest form as a metaphor for God's power.

Why was this metaphor of inversion so congenial and intimate a form of expression for the apocalyptic tradition? Does it act, following Cassirer's insight, as an expression of the mind's self-revelation? We return to this question in our conclusion.

The new vision of perfect community was embodied in the church. For Voegelin, articulating the Catholic position, the church was 'the universal spiritual organization of saints and sinners who professed faith in Christ, as the representative of the *civitas Dei* in history, as the flash of eternity into time.'[19]

The Protestant revolution, Hegel, Marx, and all that was to follow resulted, according to Voegelin, from an 'inner-Christian tension,' the bursting forth of 'components that were suppressed as heretical by the universal church.'[20] The Reformation led the way to a 'successful invasion of Western institutions by Gnostic movements,' the splitting of the universal church, and the 'gradual conquest of the political institutions in the national states.'[21] This 'Gnostic dream world,' as Voegelin calls it, became 'the civil theology of Western society.'[22]

Voegelin was correct in seeing the steady unfolding and direct line between Luther, Hegel, and Marx. Let us attempt to recapitulate very briefly this inner continuity in terms of what had been 'annulled' in each case and what had been 'preserved.'

But for those who prefer to view the apocalyptic drama of Western society in the larger context set out here, this 'inner-Christian tension' rehearsed on a much larger stage what had already taken place once before. 'These that have turned the world upside down' was, as we recall, the cry against the first of the schisms of the apocalyptic tradition.

Luther may have been the most important of 'the divine redeemers of the Gnostic empires,'[23] but the drama throughout was remarkably faithful to its underlying script. Luther affirmed the basic structure of Pauline theology around the pair of contrary terms 'lord and servant' and incorporated the previous vision of perfect community into his new view of oppressive bondage.

The cornerstone of Lutheran theology is his most important essay, 'On the Freedom of a Christian' (1520). It contrasts the paradoxical status of the Christian who is 'a perfectly free lord of all subject to none' and at the same time 'a perfectly dutiful servant of all subject to all.'[24]

The terms 'lord' and 'servant' (Herr and Knecht) are offered once more in the biblical context discussed earlier. The free Christian, following in Christ's path, and in bondage to his mortal existence, 'ought in this liberty to empty himself again' and serve his neighbour.[25] Thus the Christian servant or Knecht inverts his initial bondage to bodily existence to become free in the very service (or bondage) of his fellow man.

The characteristic second inversion takes place where the Christian servant, through faith, also becomes a lord: 'Every Christian is by faith so exalted (erhaben) above all things that, by virtue of a spiritual power, he is lord (eyn herr wirt geystlich) of all things without exception, so that nothing can do him any harm.'[26] This reiterates Paul's position, where, as we have seen, the Christian is 'lord of all' (Gal. 4:1). Lord and servant are now united in the same person within his Christian freedom. As Luther summed up the paradox at a different point: 'In Christ the lord and servant are one' (Das ynn Christo, herr und knecht eyn ding sey).[27]

Luther draws out the inner antithesis of the pair of terms lord and servant and is often led to comment more generally on the role that 'antithesis' plays in Paul: 'Antithesin facit Apostolus,'[27] the apostle creates an antithesis.[28] Luther observes as well in his debate with Erasmus: 'Scripture speaks through antithesis' and everything that is opposed to Christ reigns in him.[29] The resolution of the problem of the two opposite natures of Christ (lord and servant) was one of Luther's lifelong preoccupations, the matrix of many of his doctrines.

To lead the attack on the church, particularly on the practice of indulgences, Luther developed as his central doctrine the theology of the cross. It proved to be the theological springboard of the Protestant 'heresy.' '*Crux sola est nostra theologia,*' the cross alone is our theology, states Luther.[30] It is the true theology, the *theologia crucis*, which stands in sharp opposition to the *theologia gloria*, the theology of glory characteristic of the Catholic church. In the theology of glory, God is known by his glory, his power, and his works. But God wishes, however, to be known by the precise opposite, namely his suffering and his weakness. Hence the two natures of Christ became the theological battleground. It is to Christ's 'alien' image (*alienum*) that Luther turns, namely 'the cross, labour, all kinds of punishment, finally death and hell in the flesh.'[31] Thus, 'whoever does not take up his own cross and follow Him, is not worthy of Him, even if he were filled with all kinds of indulgences.'[32]

God's salvation follows only when man, in pursuit of Christ's alien path, reaches his low point: 'He, however, who has emptied himself [cf Phil. 2:7] through suffering no longer does works but knows that God works and does all things in him ... He knows that it is sufficient if he suffers and is brought low by the cross in order to be annihilated all the more. It is this that Christ says in John 3[:7] "You must be born anew."'[33] From the low point of man's 'annihilation' there was to emerge his salvation.

Luther's complaint against the Catholic church and against the indulgences was summed up in a familiar metaphor: 'The theology of the cross has been abrogated, and everything has been completely turned upside down' (*evacuata est theologia crucis suntque omnia plane perversa*).[34] Luther used a similar metaphor in his quarrel with the Catholic church on the confessional: '*Szo kerestu es umb unnd wilt mich zum knecht machenn ... Sihe, das ist vorkeret ding*' (Thus you turn things upside down and wish to make a slave out of me ... See, this is upside down).[35] It was one of Luther's favourite metaphors, and it had many variations.[36] Chiefly, however, it was the metaphor for transfiguring and negating the previous 'perfect community,' the Catholic church – for Luther an upside-down world.

But the power held by Luther's Supreme Being was closely akin; it was the power to set the world right-side up once more. Out of the theology of the cross there emerges a view of God's power as the *negativa essentia*, the negative essence. It is 'the negation of all things which can be felt, held and comprehended.'[37] Alternative designations of this same divine power are 'nothingness' (*Nichtigkeit*) and further, in Latin, 'nothingness and worthlessness' (*in illa ... nullitate et nihilitudine*). The origins of this doctrine are ascribed to Paul: 'For everything in us is weak and worthless: but in that nothingness and worthlessness, so to speak, God shows His strength, according to the saying (II Cor. 12:9) "My power is made perfect in weakness."'[38]

But it is the very annihilation to nothingness that is the prelude, as Luther states, to being born anew. In the essay 'On the Bondage of the Will,' the path chosen for the elect (*electos*) is 'that being humbled and brought back to nothingness by this means they may be saved.'[39]

The *negativa essentia*, God's power, is the power of inversion. A leading Lutheran scholar, Paul Althaus, sums up Luther's view of the divine power as follows: '[God] is the power that creates out of nothing or out of its opposite. It is manifested by the inversion (*Umkehrung*) of all earthly standards and relationships.'[40]

The two opposite natures of Christ were also the matrix of Luther's route to the two kingdoms, the spiritual and the worldly – but we must bypass a detailed discussion. Suffice it to say that this was the central theological problem that haunted him all his life. 'Though his nature may be two-fold,' Luther asserted, 'yet his person is not divided.'[41] How these two natures could still be one person, he thought, was ultimately 'inscrutable' and 'foolish reason' was to no avail. But in a rare and flashing insight he provided a vital clue to the paradox. We were dealing here, he stated, with the *regulae dialecticae*, the rules of dialectics.[42]

The 'dialectic of negativity' as well as the process of inversion and negation re-emerged at the heart of the Hegelian system. We can only touch briefly on some of the Lutheran doctrines of this vast philosophical enterprise. The theology of the cross was preserved in the new 'scientific' language of the Enlightenment, even while its religious form (*Vorstellung*) was annulled. Hegel stated: 'It was with Luther first of all that freedom of spirit began to exist in embryo, and its *form* indicated that it would remain in embryo.'[43] Religion had preceded philosophical science in expressing 'what spirit is.' But 'this science alone is the perfect form in which the spirit truly knows itself.'[44] Hence man's liberation was contingent on bringing to light the kernel of this religion, hidden within the outer archaic shell.

Hegel continues: 'The process of carrying forward this form of knowledge of itself is the task which spirit accomplishes as actual History.'[45] The aim of that history was to 'gain freedom and independence,' and this was achieved through 'the portentous power of the negative.'[46]

What Spirit confronted was man's physical, finite incarnation hemmed in by a material universe. This is what Hegel discerned as an 'inverted world' (verkehrte Welt), the world of sensuous perception in both its immediate and universal aspects.[47] Man's bondage lay in his finitude (Endlichkeit) and in the physical laws of the universe to which he was subject. Hegel's view of bondage related ultimately (through a circuitous route) to Paul's 'bondage under the elements of the world' (Gal. 4:3).[48] But how was the freedom from that bondage to be achieved? Hegel's answer was rooted in Luther's injunction some three centuries earlier: 'to forsake and empty ourselves, keeping nothing of our senses, but negating everything' (nos ipsos deserere et exinanire, nihil de nostro sensu retinendo, sed totum abnegando).[49]

Luther's essay 'On the Freedom of a Christian' and his theology generally provide an important key to Hegel's famous parable of lordship and bondage, the heart of The Phenomenology of Mind. Here, the prototypical slave appears 'in the form or shape of thinghood' (Gestalt der Dingheit),[50] and he is beset by 'the fear of death, the sovereign master,' i.e. the lord.[51] The parable itself is a long and enigmatic excursion, the full explication of which we must bypass here. Two essential clues however to the identity of Hegel's mysterious lord and servant come from the Old and the New Testament respectively. Hegel's text includes the sentence 'The fear of the lord is the beginning of wisdom,' an almost exact rendering of Psalm 111:10.[52] But the identity of the lord is further revealed in the New Testament. In Paul's Epistle to the Hebrews (2:15) we read: 'and deliver them who through fear of death were all their lifetime subject to bondage.' For Hegel, death, 'the sovereign master,' is the inverted form of this passage; as lord, death rules over those who are subject to his bondage.

Though death rules as the sovereign master, what precisely is his power? Luther's notion of the negativa essentia reappears in German as

Hegel's *negatives Wesen*. Thus Hegel's second indication of the power of the lord in the parable is *'die reine negative Macht, der das Ding nichts ist'* (the negative power without qualification, a power to which the thing is naught).[53]

The power of the lord is the power of the negative – a purely Lutheran position. But, as we recall, the material world of sensuous perception is, for Hegel, an 'inverted world.' Hence, the encounter of Spirit with the material, finite world is designated the 'negative of the negative,'[54] a phrase that was to be closely echoed in Marx's movement toward communism.

In another designation, Spirit is explicitly called 'this process of inversion' (*dieser Umkehrung*)[55] and is prefigured for mankind in Christ's Passion. Christ's death is explicitly called an inversion (*Umkehrung*) and serves as a paradigm for each individual where he yields up his natural will.[56]

What is the resolution of man's dilemma that Hegel offers in the parable of lordship and bondage? 'Bondage will, when completed, pass into the opposite of what it immediately is ... and change into real and true independence.'[57] It is in the self-differentiation from this world in dialectical fashion, the inward retreat, that full self-consciousness is achieved by the individual, 'the true return [of consciousness] into itself' (*Seine warhe Ruckkehr ... in sich selbst*).[58]

Thus Paul's bondage to mortality and Luther's notion of the divine power as the *negativa essentia* are brought together in Hegel. Hegel maintains: 'This is the Lutheran faith ... God is thus in spirit alone, He is not a beyond but the truest reality of the individual.'[39]

A very elaborate recasting of the Pauline proposition of the inner and outer man to be sure, but Hegel's position is ultimately a philosophical vindication of Protestant theology with its promise of Christian liberty and the Christian Kingdom. Typically, Luther's spiritual Kingdom is transfigured once more and becomes an earthly kingdom.

While self-consciousness pursues its ultimate inward retreat, man as finite being incarnates himself in the institutions of society. For Hegel, the state is 'the actuality of concrete freedom,'[60] also called 'finite' or 'secular' freedom. Here the all-embracing perfect community achieves its final historical existence: 'The private interest of its citizens is one with the common interest of the state.'[61] Hence the state, for Hegel, is the embodiment of Spirit in history, a process that unites 'the kingdom of God and the socially Moral world as one Idea.'[62] History culminates in the ideal Protestant state: 'In the Protestant state, the constitution and the code, as well as their several applications, embody the principle and the development of the moral life, which proceeds and can only proceed from the truth of religion ... and in that way ... first become actual.'[63]

This was an ideal conception of the state as embodied perfect community – Hegel's testament to the promise of the emerging liberal society. The significance of the events to which he was witness 'is known through the Spirit, for the Spirit is revealed in this history ... World-history has in it found its end.'[64]

Marx fought an unrelenting battle with theology and religion, qualified occasionally by grudging praise and perceptive insight. Much of his outlook was derivative of the Hegelian corpus of work on which he relied. He understood intimately the 'Christian dialectic' which had located man's oppression in the bondage of the body. In the debate with Max Stirner he states: 'The only reason why Christianity wanted to free us from the domination of the flesh (Herrschaft des Fleisches) ... was because it regards our flesh, our desires as something foreign to us.'[65]

Marx could even excuse partially the distorted perspectives of religion, since, as noted earlier, it had issued forth from 'an inverted world.' What was principally at stake however was a new definition of 'bondage' which Marx invoked to replace the Christian bondage to mortality (or Hegel's closely related bondage to finite existence). Man instead was in bondage to the social and economic order under which he lived. Hegel's ideal Protestant state, the paean to an evolving liberal society, was now to be turned into the new oppressive bondage, the bondage to capitalism.

Once more, as in the biblical paradigm, the argument was structured initially as a contrasting pair of terms in antithesis, namely capital and labour. Domination for Marx (Herrschaft) refers to changing forms of private property, and oppressive bondage (Knechtschaft) refers to different forms of alienated labour, entäusserte[n] Arbeit.[66] At the end of the second manuscript of *Economic and Philosophic Manuscripts of 1844*, Marx conveys in a few elliptic notes how capital and labour evolve as *Herr* and *Knecht* (lord and servant). They evolve at first in a complementary fashion, even though separate and estranged, and 'promote each other as positive conditions.' But a threshold is reached after which they develop in contradiction or opposition. The motive force of change is 'the antithesis of labour and capital' (*der Gegensatz der Arbeit und des Kapitals*).[67] It is act I of the drama which now unfolds to the typical apocalyptic climax. As Marx states, this antithesis is a 'dynamic relationship moving to its resolution.'[68]

Marx's schema, starting as it does from an alienated world where man's human essence has been completely undermined, requires to set things right through a systematic process of inversion. The mediating role is played by the proletariat. The proletariat moves from its own 'complete loss of humanity and can only redeem itself through the total redemption of humanity'; the German text contrasts *völlige[r] Verlust* (complete loss) and *völlige Wiedergewinnung* (complete redemption).[69] A dehumanized and enslaved proletariat becomes a redeemed proletariat. Recalling that the proletariat is Marx's *Knecht* or slave, we see here the characteristic inversion from oppressive to exalted bondage.

The exalted bondage now goes through the second inversion, and the exalted 'slave' becomes a 'lord.' Marx refers several times in *Communist Manifesto* to the 'lordship' of the proletariat – its *Herrschaft* or supremacy. His graphic instruction reads: 'The first step in the revolution by the working class is to raise the proletariat to the position of ruling class.'[70] This differed little in its rhetoric from Moses' promise to the Jews: 'And the Lord shall make thee the head, and not the tail; and thou shalt be above only, and thou shalt not be beneath' (Deut. 28:13). Compare as well Paul's expression 'for in nothing am I behind the very chiefest apostles, though I be nothing' (II Cor. 12:11) (in Luther's translation: *da ich doch nicht weniger bin, als die hohen Apostel sind, wiewohl ich nichts bin*). It had close echoes in Marx's ringing challenge, the 'revolutionary boldness which flings at its adversary the defiant phrase: I am nothing and I should be everything' (*Ich bin nichts, und ich müsste alles sein*).[71]

For Marx, capitalism was pictured as an upside-down world at its most extreme. '*Everything,*' Marx stated, '*appears upside down in competition.'*[72] But in attempting to set the world right-side up once more, Marx fell back on a rhetoric of striking similarity to everything he disavowed: Hegel, Luther, and the Bible were all characteristically present in the mode in which man would now once more 'invert' his bondage and move to yet another version of the perfect community.

Lodged within this evolving antithesis is a vast and complex network of social and economic development to which I can hardly do justice here. But some suggestive notions can be offered of the way that Marx viewed money, capitalist economic relations, and the course of revolution.

Money, for Marx, is 'the alienated ability of mankind.'[73] It is designated by Marx 'this overturning power' (*diese verkehrende Macht*), and he elaborates on money's peculiar inverting properties. Money is 'the general overturning (*allgemeine Verkehrung*) of individualities which turns them into their contrary (*in ihr Gegenteil umkehrt*) and adds contradictory attributes to the attributes.'[74]

In *Grundrisse*, the same tendency proves to be characteristic of the capitalist mode of production in general. Marx notes: 'Inversion (*Verkehrung*) is the foundation of the capitalist mode of production, not only of its distribution.' He states: 'This twisting and inversion (*Verdrehung und Verkehrung*) is the *real* [phenomenon], not a merely *supposed one* existing merely in the imagination of the workers and the capitalists.'[75]

As this notion emerges in the fully developed version of *Capital*, Marx maintains that 'capitalist production begets, with the inexorability of a law of nature, its own negation. It is the negation of negation.'[76] Further, 'it is evident that the laws of appropriation or of private property ... become by their own inner and inexorable dialectic changed into their very opposite.'[77]

The Hegelian and Lutheran influence of 'negation' and 'inversion' persists through both the early and the mature Marx. Emancipation will come about as the result of 'the formation of a class with radical chains ... a class that is the dissolution of all classes, a sphere of society having a universal character because of its universal suffering ... because ... unqualified wrong is perpetrated on it.'[78] The proletariat already embodies 'the negative result of society' and (in a characteristic reversal) 'merely elevates into a principle of society what society had advanced as the principle of the proletariat,' namely, 'the negation of private property.'[79] The call for revolution in *Communist Manifesto* was a call to invert historical development as it had proceeded thus far (umgekehreten Verhältnis zur geschichtlichen Entwicklung).[80]

There are characteristic words in Marx that capture this apocalyptic resolution, the abrupt leap or inversion where the underlying contradiction is suspended and transformed into its opposite. Communism, as man's total salvation, will happen '"all at once" and simultaneously' (auf einmal).[81] One of Marx's favourite words is *Umschlag*, 'the turn into its opposite.'[82] He refers also to *dieser dialektische Umschlag* (the dialectical reversal).[83]

This use of language is reminiscent of one of Luther's characteristic words, umbkeren (to overturn or invert): 'Our Lord God can immediately overturn things despite the Emperor or the Pope' (*Unser Herr Gott kans bald umbkeren trotz Keiser, Bapst*).[84]

We will recall as well that out of Luther's battle with the Catholic church, where 'everything has been completely turned upside-down,' there emerged the theology of the cross, centred on God's power as the *negativa essentia*, the power of inversion. Marx, in turn, regarded capitalism as 'an enchanted, perverted (read "inverted"), topsy-turvy world' (die verzauberte, verkehrte und auf den Kopf gestellte Welt),[85] but communism 'overturns the basis of all earlier relations of production and exchange.'[86]

The apocalyptic resolution of perfect community is recapitulated in Marx in the explicit abolition of power. Political power, Marx claims, is merely the result of class antagonisms, and with the abolition of the latter, a society will evolve where 'there will be no further political power as such.'[87] In a well-known passage from *Communist Manifesto*, he reiterates this notion:

When, in the course of development, class distinctions have disappeared, and all production has been concentrated in the hands of a vast association of the whole nation, the public power will lose its political character. Political power, properly so called, is merely the organized power of one class for oppressing another. If the proletariat during its contest with the bourgeoisie is compelled, by the force of circumstances, to organize itself as a class, if, by means of a revolution, it makes itself the ruling class, and, as such, sweeps away by force the old conditions of production, then it will, along with these conditions, have swept away the conditions for the existence of class antagonisms, and of classes generally, and will thereby have abolished its own supremacy as a class.[88]

The German text of this last clause reads *hebt ... damit seine eigene Herrschaft als Klasse auf*.[89] Compare this with Paul's prescription for the kingdom of God, when Christ 'shall have put down all rule and all authority and power' (I Cor. 15:24) (in Luther's translation [1546]: *Wenn er auffheben wird alle herrschaft, und alle oberkeit und Gewalt*).

This comparison reveals the characteristic culmination of the apocalyptic vision. In its rhetorical structure, Marx's socialism is as comprehensive and all-embracing a vision of community as the 'holy nation' of the Old Testament, as the *totus Christus* of the New Testament, as Luther's spiritual kingdom or Hegel's ideal Protestant state. This final version of socialism repeats the classical and systematic process of inversion of the basic antithesis of lordship and bondage. It promises, once more, perfect community without power and conflict.

III

In the short compass of this paper I have tried to deal not with the substantive doctrines of some of the main expressions of the apocalyptic tradition or with its 'truths' but with its forms and the structures of its rhetoric. These have been remarkably consistent over three millennia. We have the positing of the contrasting pair of opposites, lord and servant, and, subsequently, the resolution of this opposition through negation and inversion into a vision of perfect community. It is this characteristic rhetorical structure that has given to the apocalyptic tradition its intimate and arresting appeal.

But it is also on this very same structure and vocabulary that schism invariably drew. This negation of the previous vision of perfect community became, in Rosemary Reuther's language, the left hand of the new round of self-affirmation in yet another vision of perfect community.

Each such vision attempts to write 'finis' to history. On the theistic side, the kingdom is 'beyond history,' as decreed in Revelation; on the secular side, history itself is suspended, as in Hegel and Marx. Yet for those who wish to appraise the more limited and finite question of the unfolding of the apocalyptic tradition within history, both camps can be seen as labouring under a dramatic blind spot. By foreclosing history in their different ways, they fail to anticipate the extraordinary internal momentum yet to surge forth in the next round, already, if invisibly, in a state of gestation.

In my view, the evidence is consistent. Schism is inherent in the apocalyptic tradition, a latent force virtually as powerful as that of the given doctrinal orthodoxy. It is difficult to distinguish the language that leads to perfect community from the language that leads away from it to yet another characteristic embodiment; inversion and negation in their various forms and expressions are the characteristic rhetorical mode of both. Hence we must assign a far more significant place to the role of schismatic movements within the heart of this tradition since they form a consistent and integral part of its millennial history.

The postulate of the ultimate cosmic unity of God's and man's intentions (in theological language), or the total harmony of the state with the intrinsic goals of the proletariat (in the communist version), contains within it the fatal rift for those who live in history. Sooner or later must come the revelation of an abyss that can be bridged only by yet another schism, an apocalyptic trajectory (or springboard) to a new cosmic harmony. A new vision of domination and oppression is proclaimed and then perceived and 'felt.'

However 'dialectically' we tend to see such an unfolding, the height of utopianism is contained in the expectation that society on the one side and (dialectical) consciousness on the other can move in tandem in compatible forms. The resultant strain between the two, building to a dramatic threshold, is the ultimate source of the new schism. In the train of the new vision, there moves forward yet another 'perfect community,' the quintessential catalyst of political mobilization. The depth of present injustice awaits its inversion into yet another round of perfection.

What role does the hidden structure of human consciousness play in the formulation of this vision? What role does it play in generating the seeds of this vision's schismatic fate? We can do little more here than attempt to establish this question on the present agenda of modernity.

The acceptance of such a question does not imply either a new determinism or the assumption that consciousness alone is all there is. Such a question attempts only to identify the mediating role that consciousness exercises in this millennial cycle.

In theological language, the only assumption that need be made here is the fallibility or imperfection inherent in the human perception and transmission of divine revelation. To assume the opposite would indeed be presumptuous. But the question now being put is whether such fallibility or imperfection in human consciousness is necessarily a random or fortuitous affair. Is it indeed possible that there is order and consistency in the structure, that is, in the very limitations of human consciousness?

Voegelin vents much of his wrath on those engaged, in gnostic fashion, in immanentizing the eschaton – that is, in locating the divine spirit and its promise within human consciousness.[90] The prior and more limited question raised here, however, separates the issue of the human structure of that consciousness from the events of Revelation. The theological debate around gnosticism unites the two issues and thus obscures the shape of the finite.

In Marxist language, the same question comes up in a radically different perspective. How do we account for the extraordinary consistency of this mode of perception of 'domination and oppression' and the mode of its resolution? This occurs, as we have seen, in widely different settings over three millennia, amid very different class structures and very different relations to the ownership of the means of production. Even though, as Marx states, the ideologists of bourgeois society 'inevitably put the thing upside-down' (auf den Kopf stellen),[91] the similarity of the 'image' being inverted is unmistakeable.

From theism and Marxism a common issue begins to arise in our present confrontation with modernity. One of the crucial features of modernity is the reiteration of the imperious and resonant expectations of consciousness, running toward perfection along its apocalyptic track. This recurs persistently despite the inertia of our economic and political institutions, with which it is in collision. In the complex undergrowth of bureaucratic and technological systems, the demands of co-ordination, stability, growth, and even equity generate internal momenta of their own. These are often contradictory and antithetical to the pristine harmonies and dialectics of the apocalyptic mode of thought. Both the Pauline and Marxian views of power that were cited above are only one illustration of temporal innocence.

The proliferation of left-wing and liberation movements in the last decade and a half has exhibited even more vigorous schismatic tendencies than we had seen previously. Marcuse and the radical movements of our own day are no less the unexpected (and, to some, unwelcome) heirs of the apocalyptic tradition than their millennial forebears. They reincarnate the old apocalyptic legacy of 'domination and oppression' and charge once more into the anonymous tyranny of our bureaucracies, despite the doctrinal 'birth control' of the established left and the cries of heresy and excommunication. Yet the recent outcome of these liberation movements had a more transient character than ever before. A sense of futility now haunts these apocalyptic step-children.

We cannot hope to deal with the issues they raise as long as we remain innocent of the hidden relation of the apocalyptic tradition to human consciousness. Our continuing commitment to this tradition in the largest sense has rooted within it the seeds of periodic eruption as we re-echo in doctrinal forms the latent structures of the mind. Hence Voegelin's focus on the 'inner-Christian tension,' the struggle with heresy in the universal church, and the powerful momentum of gnosticism in Western society can be regarded as one phase of a still larger question.

The problem that was suspended almost two millennia ago has now been forced upon us by this encounter of the apocalyptic tradition with modernity. Jesus had stated to Pilate: 'My kingdom is not of this world: if my kingdom were of this world, then would my servants fight' (John 18:36). Two thousand years later we can no longer fail to recognize the enduring reality of the biblical legacy in history – in 'this world.'

In writing recently about Simone Weil, George Grant charted a course that each of us may pursue in his own way: 'Just because western Christianity has realized its destiny of becoming secularized, it is essential to tear oneself free of the causes of that destiny, without removing oneself from the necessities of our present or from the reality of Christ.'[92]

The causes of that 'destiny' lie in the projection of the inner structure of human consciousness. Its articulation, in all its inspired, recurring brilliance, forms the history of the apocalyptic tradition in Western society. But now, in the fulness of its millennial history, the forms of this tradition have now to be reviewed – or more appropriately, *aufgehoben*. It was Hegel who first pointed us toward the last dark continent of the mind. That, in my view, remains the quest of our time.

NOTES

1 George Grant *Technology and Empire, Perspectives on North America*, (Toronto: House of Anansi 1969) 88.

   This paper draws on the results of a research project made possible through the generosity of the Walter and Duncan Gordon Foundation. An initial paper, 'The Apocalyptic Tradition: Luther and Marx,' was presented to the conference on Political Theology in the Canadian Context at the School of Religious Studies, University of Saskatchewan, 9–11 March 1977. The proceedings of this conference will be published under the editorship of Professor B.G. Smillie. I have drawn on much of the same research for the present paper, but addressed it to a somewhat different theme. My debt to many friends and to my research assistants will be acknowledged in a forthcoming book.

2 Eric Voegelin *The New Science of Politics: An Introduction* (Chicago: University of Chicago Press 1952) 176

3 Ibid 106

4 Michael Polanyi *Personal Knowledge: Towards a Post-Critical Philosophy* (London: Routledge and Kegan Paul 1958) 233–9

5 Reinhold Niebuhr *The Irony of American History* (New York: Scribner's 1952) 163

6 Karl Marx *Critique of Hegel's 'Philosophy of Right'* ed J. O'Malley (Cambridge: Cambridge University Press 1970) 131; this will be cited subsequently as O'Malley *Critique. Frühe Schriften* I ed H.J. Lieber and P. Furth (Stuttgart: Cotta Verlag 1962).

7 Karl Marx and Frederick Engels *The German Ideology* (Moscow: Progress Publishers 1964) 37; this will be cited subsequently as *GI*.

8 I have expanded at greater length on this intermediate process in my forthcoming paper 'The Apocalyptic Tradition: Luther and Marx,' referred to in note 1, above.

9 Ernst Cassirer *Language and Myth* (New York: Dover Publications 1953)

10 L.S. Vygotsky *Thought and Language* (Cambridge, Mass: M.I.T. Press 1962) 153

11 Claude Lévi-Strauss *From Honey to Ashes* (London: Jonathan Cape 1973) 473. Cf also *The Elementary Structures of Kinship* (London: Eyre and Spottiswoode 1969) 84, for 'certain fundamental structures of the human mind.'

12 Claude Lévi-Strauss *Structural Anthropology* I (New York: Basic Books 1963) 21

13 Claude Lévi-Strauss *L'Homme nu* (Paris: Plon 1971) 611

14 Claude Lévi-Strauss *Totemism* (Boston: Beacon Press 1963) 90

15 André Akoun et al 'The Father of Structural Anthropology – A Conversation with C. Lévi-Strauss' *Psychology Today*, 5:12 (May 1972) 76

16 Rosemary R. Reuther *Faith and Fratricide: The Theological Roots of Anti-Semitism* (New York: Seabury 1974) 228

17 Ibid 229

18 *Wir die religiöse Vorstellung in Gedanken fassen* in G.W.F. Hegel *Werke* (Berlin: Duncker und Humblot 1840–7) IX 25; this edition will be cited subsequently as *Werke*. Cf *The Philosophy of History* trans J. Sibree, Dover Publications (New York: Dover 1956) 20; this will be cited subsequently as *Phil Hist*.

19 Eric Voegelin *The New Science* 109

20 Ibid 107

21 Ibid 134

22 Ibid 161, 178

23 Ibid 131

24 J.J. Pelikan and H.T. Lehman *Luther's Works; American Edition* (St Louis and Philadelphia: Muhlenberg 1955–) XXXI 344; this edition will be cited subsequently as *LW*. The German edition of Luther's work used here is *D. Martin Luthers Werke: Kritische Gesammtausgabe* (Weimar 1883–); this edition will be cited as *WA* (Luther's spelling is retained in the original which often differs from modern German).

25 *Debet tamen rursus se exinanire hac in libertate ...* (*WA* VII 65). Cf also *evacuator a seipso*, *WA* II 564. Luther inverts the term for servant and slave, *Knecht*, in precisely the same way as the equivalent *eved* in the Old Testament and *doulos* in the New Testament. *Knecht* is in fact Luther's translation for both the Hebrew and Greek terms.

26 *LW* XXXI 354; *WA* VII 27

27 *WA* XVIII 327

28 *WA* LVI 366. Cf *Observanda autem hic est Antithesis*, *WA* XL pt 2 423; also ibid 409, 414.

29 *Si Scripturas per contentionem loqui concedis ...* *WA* XVIII 779. Gerhard Ebeling comments: 'Luther's thought always contains an antithesis, tension between

strongly opposed but related polarities'; *Luther: An Introduction to His Thought* trans R.A. Wilson (Philadelphia: Fortress 1970) 25.

30 *WA* v 176

31 *LW* xxxi

32 Ibid 255

33 Ibid 55

34 Ibid 225; *WA* i 613

35 *WA* viii 157

36 In relation to *umbkeren*, to overturn, the editors of Luther's works comment: '*Sehr oft bei Luther*' (frequently found in Luther); *WA* xxxiv pt 2 317 note 1.

37 *LW* xxv 383

38 *LW* v 227; *WA* xliii 585. Cf 'the Lord of all who is the same as nothing'; *LW* v 219.

39 *Ut, isto modo humiliati et in nihilum redacti, salvi fiant; WA* xviii 633

40 *Sie ist die Macht, aus dem Nichts, aus dem Gegenteil zu schaffen. Sie erweist sich gerade in der Umkehrung aller irdischen Massstäbe und Verhältnisse;* Paul Althaus *Die Theologie Martin Luthers* (Gütersloh: Gütersloher Verlagshaus, Gerd Mohn 1962) 41

41 *Duplex quidem est natura, sed persona non est divisa; WA* xliii 580

42 *WA* xxxiv pt 2 279

43 *Hegel's Lectures on The History of Philosophy* trans E.S. Haldane and F.H. Simson (London: Routledge and Kegan Paul 1896, reprinted 1955) iii 148, my italics. This will be cited subsequently as *Hist Phil.*

44 *The Phenomenology of Mind* trans J.B. Baillie (New York: Harper Torchbooks 1967) 801; this edition will be cited subsequently as *Phen*. The German edition used here is *Phänomenologie des Geistes* (Frankfurt: Suhrkamp Verlag 3, 1970); this will be cited subsequently as *Phän*.

45 *Phen* 801

46 *Phen* 93. Cf *die ungeheure Macht des Negativen; Phän* 36.

47 Cf 'The changeless kingdom of laws, the immediate ectype and copy of the world of perception'; *Phen* 203; also 207.

48 Hegel uses the word 'finite' in apposition to the word 'evil': 'the natural ... the finite, evil, in fact is destroyed'; *Lectures on the Philosophy of Religion* trans E.B. Speirs and J.B. Sanderson (Trübner, London: Kegan Paul, Trench 1895) iii 96; this will be cited subsequently as *Phil Rel.* Cf as well finitude (*Endlichkeit*), used synonymously with externality or outwardness (*Äusserlichkeit*), otherness or other-being (*Anderseyn*), and imperfection (*Unvollkommenheit*); *Werke* xii 330. The

imperfection attributed to finitude consists in the fact that man 'can exist in a way which is not in conformity with (his) inner substantial nature ... his inwardness'; *Phil Rel* III 123. In 'the language of faith,' Hegel's statement on finitude runs as follows: 'Christ assumed [human] finitude, finitude *(Endlichkeit)* in all its forms, which is the final tapering point of evil *(das Böse ist ...)*'; *Werke* XII 301, my translation. Cf *Phil Rel* III 92–3.

49 *WA* I 29

50 *Phen* 234; *Phän* 150

51 *Phen* 237

52 *Phen* 238. Cf also Job 28:28 and Proverbs 9:10.

53 *Phän* 152; *Phen* 236. In other designations Hegel refers to the lord as 'absolute universal Being as ... mere nothingness' *(allgemeine Wesen als der Nichtigkeit)*, in *Phen* 263, *Phän* 173; 'the negative essence' *(negatives Wesen)* or simply 'nothingness' *(Nichtigkeit)*, in *Phen* 225, *Phän* 143. Cf also 'absolute negativity' in *Phen* 233, 237; 'absolute negation of this existence' in *Phen* 246; and 'absolute negation' in *Phen* 226.

54 *Phil Rel* III 91 note 1. Cf also 'Spirit ... constructs not merely one world, but a twofold world, divided and self-opposed'; *Phen* 510.

55 *Phil Rel* II 255; *Werke* XII 125

56 *Werke* XII 303

57 *Phen* 237

58 *Phen* 251; *Phän* 163. Cf H.G. Gadamer *Hegel's Dialectic: Five Hermeneutical Studies* trans P.C. Smith (Yale University Press 1976) 53: 'We must now grasp that the "inverted world" is in fact the real world'; also 67: 'Hegel's dialectical analysis ... seeks out the dialectical reversal within the self-consciousness of the master.'

59 *Hist Phil* III 159

60 *Hegel's Philosophy of Right* trans T.M. Knox (New York: Oxford University Press 1967) 160

61 *Phil Hist* 24

62 Ibid 380

63 *Hegel's Philosophy of Mind* trans W. Wallace (Oxford: Oxford University Press 1971) 291

64 *Hist Phil* III 16

65 *GI* 274. *Karl Marx, Friederich Engels Werke* (Berlin: Dietz Verlag) III 237; this edition of Marx's work will be cited subsequently as *MEW*.

66 Karl Marx, *Economic and Philosophic Manuscripts of 1844* ed D.J. Struik, trans Martin Milligan (New York: International Publishers 1964) 118; this will be cited subsequently as *EPM*. *Frühe Schriften* I 574

67 *EPM* 132; *Frühe Schriften* I 590

68 *EPM* 132

69 O'Malley *Critique* 141–2; *Frühe Schriften* I 503–4

70 Karl Marx and Frederick Engels *Selected Works* 2 vols (Moscow: Foreign Languages Publishing House 1958) I 51, 53; this will be cited subsequently as *Selected Works*. *Frühe Schriften* II 839, 842

71 O'Malley *Critique* 140; *Frühe Schriften* I 501

72 Karl Marx *Capital: A Critique of Political Economy* 3 vols trans S. Moore and E. Aveling (Chicago: C.H. Kerr 1906) III 244; this will be cited subsequently as *Capital*. *Es Erscheint also in der Konkurrenz alles verkehrt, MEW* XXV 219

73 *EPM* 168

74 *EPM* 169; *Frühe Schriften* I 635

75 Karl Marx *Grundrisse: Foundations of the Critique of Political Economy* trans Martin Nicolaus, (New York: Vintage 1973) 831; this will be cited subsequently as *Grundrisse*. The German edition is *Grundrisse der Kritik der politischen Ökonomie* (Rohentwurf) (Berlin: Dietz Verlag 1953) 715–16.

76 *Capital* I 837

77 *Capital* I 639

78 O'Malley *Critique* 141

79 Ibid 142

80 *Selected Works* I 63; *Frühe Schriften* II 855

81 *GI* 47; *MEW* III 35

82 *Grundrisse* 674; cf Martin Nicolaus's Introduction, 32. I do not include here the financial or accounting usage of *Umschlag* meaning 'turnover' as used in *Capital*.

83 *MEW* XXIII 610 note 23; *Capital* I 640 note 1

84 *WA* XXXIII 348

85 *Capital* III 966; *MEW* XXV 838

86 *GI* 86

87 *MEW* IV 182; my translation. The full passage reads: 'In the course of its development to replace the old bourgeois society, the working class will establish an association that excludes classes and their antagonism (*Gegensatz*), and there will be no further political power as such; since it is political power that is the official expression of class antagonism within the bourgeois society.' Cf *The Poverty of*

Philosophy (Moscow: Progress Publishers 1973) 151. Compare also: 'The communist revolution abolishes the rule (*Herrschaft*) of all classes with the classes themselves'; *GI* 85; *MEW* III 70.

88 *Selected Works* I 54. A similar passage in Engels's *Socialism, Utopian and Scientific* reads as follows: '*The proletariat seizes political power and turns the means of production into state property.* But, in doing this, it abolishes itself as proletariat, abolishes all class distinctions and class antagonisms, abolishes also the state as state ... When at last it becomes the real representative of the whole of society, it renders itself unnecessary'; *Selected Works* II 150.

89 *Frühe Schriften* II 843

90 Eric Voegelin *The New Science* 163–6: 'The immanentization of the Christian eschaton made it possible to endow society in its natural existence with a meaning which Christianity denied to it. And the totalitarianism of our time must be understood as journey's end of the Gnostic search for a civil theology' (163).

91 *GI* 462; *MEW* III 405

92 Toronto *Globe and Mail* (12 Feb. 1977) 43

Bibliography of George Grant

BOOKS

Philosophy in the Mass Age. Toronto: Copp Clark 1959; New York: Hill and
   Wang 1960
Lament for a Nation. Toronto: McClelland and Stewart 1965
Technology and Empire. Toronto: Anansi 1969
Time as History. (The Massey Lectures, 1969) Toronto: Canadian Broadcasting
   Corporation 1971
English-Speaking Justice. (The Wood Lectures, 1974) Sackville, NB: Mount
   Allison University Press 1977

PARTS OF BOOKS

'Dennis Lee – Poetry and Philosophy' in *Tasks of Passion: Dennis Lee at Mid-
   Career*. K. Mulhallen, D. Bennet, R. Brown, eds. Toronto: Descant Editions
   1982. 229–35
'Technology and Empire' in *Philosophy and Technology*. Robert Mackey and
   Carl Mitcham, eds. New York: The Free Press 1972 (a retitled reprint of 'In
   Defense of North America' from *Technology and Empire*)

With Sheila Grant

'Abortion and Rights' in *The Right to Birth: Some Christian Views on Abor-
   tion*. Eugene Fairweather and Ian Gentles, eds. Toronto: The Anglican
   Book Centre 1976. 1–12
'Euthanasia' in *Care for the Dying and Bereaved*. Ian Gentles ed. Toronto: The
   Anglican Book Centre 1982. 133–43

ARTICLES AND PAMPHLETS

Canada: An Introduction to a Nation. Toronto: Canadian Institute of International Affairs (Special Series) 1943. Five subsequent editions (1943–6)

The Empire: Yes or No? Toronto: Ryerson Press 1945

'Have We a Canadian Nation?' *Public Affairs* (Institute of Public Affairs, Dalhousie University) 1945. 873: 161–5

'Philosophy,' *Royal Commission Studies* (The Massey Report), 119–33. Ottawa: King's Printer

'The Pursuit of an Illusion: A Commentary on Bertrand Russell,' *Dalhousie Review* 32: 97–109 (summer 1952)

'Philosophy and Adult Education,' *Food for Thought* (Toronto) 14: 3–8 (Sept.–Oct. 1953)

'Two Languages in the Ethical Tradition – Hebrew and Greek.' An address delivered to the Maritime Philosophical Association 1953. Mimeo 5 pp (published in the *United Churchman*, Sackville NB 1953)

'Plato and Popper,' *Canadian Journal of Economic and Political Science*, 20: 185–94 (Sept.–Oct. 1954)

'Adult Education in an Expanding Economy,' *Food for Thought* (Toronto) 15: 4–10 (Sept.–Oct. 1954)

Entries on Canadian history in *Chambers Encyclopaedia*, various volumes. London: Newnes 1955.

The Paradox of Democratic Education. The Ansley Memorial Lecture, Assumption College (now the University of Windsor), Windsor, Ontario, 1955. Published by the Ontario Secondary School Teachers Federation, Toronto.

'Jean-Paul Sartre,' in *Architects of Modern Thought* (1st and 2nd series), ed. John A. Irving. Toronto: Canadian Broadcasting Corporation Publications 1955. 39–45

'Contemplation in an Expanding Economy,' in *The Anglican Outlook* (Montreal) 10/7: 8–10 (May 1955) (a reprint of 'Adult Education in an Expanding Economy')

'The Uses of Freedom – a word in our world,' *Queen's Quarterly* 65: 515–27 (winter 1956)

'The Minds of Men in the Atomic Age,' *Texts and Addresses Delivered at the Twenty-Fourth Annual Couchiching Conference* (Toronto: Canadian Institute on Public Affairs) 1955. 39–45

'Philosophy,' *Encyclopedia Canadiana* (The Grolier Society of Canada 1958) 8: 184–9

'Fyodor Dostoevsky,' in *Architects of Modern Thought* (3rd and 4th series), ed. John A. Irving. Toronto: Canadian Broadcasting Corporation Publications 1959. 71–83

'An Ethic of Community,' in *Social Purpose for Canada*, ed. Michael Oliver. Toronto: University of Toronto Press 1961. 3–26

'Philosophy and Religion,' in *The Great Ideas Today*, eds. Mortimer J. Adler and Robert M. Hutchins. Chicago: Encyclopaedia Britannica, Inc. 1961. 337–76

'Conceptions of Health,' in *Psychiatry and Responsibility*, eds. Helmut Schoeck and James W. Wiggins. Princeton: Van Nostrand 1962. 117–34

'Carl Gustav Jung,' in *Architects of Modern Thought* (5th and 6th series), ed. John A. Irving. Toronto: Canadian Broadcasting Corporation Publications 1962. 63–74

'Tyranny and Wisdom – the controversy between L. Strauss and A. Kojève,' *Social Research* 31: 45–72 (1963)

'Religion and the State,' *Queen's Quarterly*, 70: 183–7 (summer 1963)

'Value and Technology,' *Canadian Conference on Social Welfare: Proceedings* (Ottawa: Queen's Printer 1964). 21–9

'Progrès, technique et valeurs humaines,' *Canadian Conference on Social Welfare: Proceedings* 30–9 (French translation of 'Value and Technology')

'Turning New Leaves,' *Canadian Forum* XLVIII: 282–3 (March 1964)

'Protest and Technology,' in *Revolution and Response*, ed. Charles Hanly. Toronto: McClelland and Stewart 1966. 122–8

'A Critique of the New Left,' in *Canada and Radical Social Change*, ed. D.I. Roussopoulos. Toronto: McClelland and Stewart 1966. 55–61

'Canadian Fate and Imperialism,' *Canadian Dimension* 4, #3: 21–5 (March, April 1967)

Comments on the Great Society in *Great Societies and Quiet Revolutions* (The Thirty-Fifth Annual Couchiching Conference), ed. John Irwin. Toronto: Canadian Institute on Public Affairs and Canadian Broadcasting Corporation 1967. 71–6

'Wisdom in the Universities: Part One,' *This Magazine Is About Schools* 1, #4: 70–85 (1967)

'The University Curriculum,' *This Magazine Is About Schools* 2, #5: 52–7 (winter 1968) (continuation of 'Wisdom in the Universities')

'A Conversation on Technology,' with Gad Horowitz, *Journal of Canadian Studies* 4, #3: 3–6 (Aug. 1969)

'Is Freedom Man's Only Meaning?' *Saturday Night* (Toronto) 84: 31–3 (March 1969) (excerpts from *Technology and Empire*)

'Horowitz and Grant Talk,' *Canadian Dimension* 6: 18–20 (Dec.–Jan. 1969–70)

'Revolution and Tradition,' *Canadian Forum* 50: 88–93 (April–May 1970)

'Nationalism and Rationality,' *Canadian Forum* 50: 336–7 (Jan. 1971) (also translated into French for *Le Devoir*)

'Revolution and Tradition,' in *Tradition and Revolution*, ed. Lionel Rubinoff. Toronto: Macmillan 1971. 81–95 (reprint with alterations of 'Revolution and Tradition')

New introduction to *Lament For a Nation* in Carleton Library Edition. Toronto: McClelland and Stewart 1971

'Ideology in Modern Empires,' in *Perspectives of Empire: Essays Presented to Gerald S. Graham*, ed. J.E. Flint and G. Williams. London: Longman's Group 1973. 189–97

'Canadian Fate and Imperialism,' in *The Evolution of Canadian Literature in English 1945–1970*, ed. Mary Jane Edwards, George Parker, and Patrick Denham. Toronto: Holt, Rinehart & Winston 1973. 100–9

'Knowing and Making,' *Transactions of the Royal Society of Canada* (4th series, number 12, 1974), 59–67

'The University Curriculum and the Technological Threat,' in *The Sciences and the Humanities and the Technological Threat*, ed. William Roy Niblett. London: University of London Press, 21–35

'The Computer Does Not Impose on Us the Ways It Should Be Used,' in *Beyond Industrial Growth* (Massey College Lectures, 1974–5), ed. Abraham Rotstein. Toronto: University of Toronto Press 1976. 117–31

'On National Unity,' in *Grant and Lamontagne on National Unity*, a pamphlet published by Constellation Life Assurance Company 1977. 5–9

Introduction to *The Liberal Idea of Canada* by James and Robert Laxer. Toronto: James Lorimer 1977. 9–12

'Can We Think outside Technology?' Tract no. 24, Brighton: Gryphon Press, University of Sussex 1977. 5–23

'Faith and the Multiversity,' in *The Search for Absolute Values in a Changing World*, 1 (Proceedings of the Sixth International Conference on the Unity of the Sciences, San Francisco, 1977), 183–94

'Diefenbaker: A democrat in Theory and in Soul,' Toronto: *Globe and Mail,*
23 Aug. 1979, 7
'Nietzsche and the Ancients: Philosophy and Scholarship,' *Dionysius* III: 5–16
(Dec. 1979)
'Homage to Celine,' to be published in *Queen's Quarterly* (fall 1983)

Appendix

Critique of much of the above is found in:
George Grant in Process: Essays and Conversations, ed. Larry Schmidt.
Toronto: Anansi 1978

BOOK REVIEWS

H.M. Tory by E.A. Corbett. *Canadian Forum* (Aug. 1954): 112–13
*Church and State in Canada West: Three Studies on the Relation of Denomi-
nationalism and Nationalism, 1841–1867,* in *Journal of Ecclesiastical
History* XII: 131 (1961)
Thought – From the Learned Societies of Canada by W.J. Gage, *Dialogue* I
(1962) 100–1
The Predicament of Democratic Man by E. Cahn. *University of Toronto Law
Journal* (1964): 461–3
The Four Faces of Peace by L.B. Pearson. *Canadian Forum* (Sept. 1964): 140
The Secular City by Harvey Cox. *United Church Observer* (1 July 1966): 16, 27
The Technological Society by Jacques Ellul. *Canadian Dimension* (May 1966):
59–60
*The Collected Works of Walter Bagehot, Volumes V–VIII: The Political
Writings,* ed. Norman St John Stevas. *Globe and Mail* (1 March 1975): 31
The Gladstone Diaries, vols. III and IV: 1840–1847, 1848–1854, eds. R.D.
Foot and H.C.G. Matthew. *Globe and Mail* (20 Sept. 1975): 35
Nietzsche's View of Socrates by W.J. Dannhauser. *American Political Science
Review* (summer 1977): 1127–9
Simone Weil by Simone Petrement, trans Raymond Rosenthal. *Globe and
Mail* (12 Feb. 1977): 43
Torture in Greece: The First Torturer's Trial, 1975, by Amnesty International.
Globe and Mail (11 June 1977): 42–3

Essays on Politics and Society by John Stuart Mill in *Collected Works*, vols.
    XVIII and XIX, textual ed. J.M. Robson. *Globe and Mail* (6 Aug. 1977): 42
The Great Code: The Bible and Literature by Northrop Frye. *Globe and Mail*
    (27 Feb. 1982): E 17
Outsiders: A Study in Life and Letters by H. Mayer. *Globe and Mail* (16 Oct.
    1982): E 16
The World, The Text and the Critic, by E.W. Said. *Globe and Mail* (7 May
    1983): E 18

Contributors

Alex Colville	Artist, Wolfville, Nova Scotia
Dennis Lee	Poet, essayist, editor
Eugene Combs	Professor, Department of Religious Studies, and Associate Dean of Social Sciences (Studies), McMaster University, Hamilton, Ontario
James Doull	Professor, Department of Classics, Dalhousie University, Halifax, Nova Scotia
John G. Arapura	Professor, Department of Religious Studies, McMaster University
Jan Yün-hua	Professor, Department of Religious Studies, McMaster University
Wilfred Cantwell Smith	Professor of the Comparative History of Religion, and Chairman, The Study of Religion, Harvard University, Cambridge, Mass
Terence Penelhum	Professor, Department of Philosophy and Religious Studies, University of Calgary
Abraham Rotstein	Professor, Department of Economics, University of Toronto